W9-BLM-058

INTERIOR DESIGN

SOLUTIONS

20 *ready-made room schemes*
for your home

RUTH PRETTY

WARD LOCK

BOCA RATON PUBLIC LIBRARY
BOCA RATON, FLORIDA

*To my dear husband Bill – for swapping adventures on the high seas
for the company of a rather crotchety author*

ACKNOWLEDGEMENTS
I am deeply indebted to the late David Hicks for being so extraordinarily generous with his time
and amazing talent and for allowing pictures of his work to appear in this book.
My heartfelt thanks also to interior designer Stephen Ryan, photographer John Spragg and
everyone at Cassells for their unstinting help.

A WARD LOCK BOOK
First published in the UK 1999 by Ward Lock
Wellington House, 125 Strand, London WC2R 0BB
A Cassell Imprint

Copyright © Text Ruth Pretty 1997, 1999
Copyright © Illustrations Ward Lock 1997

Some parts first published in the UK 1997 as
The Ultimate Interior Designer

Edited by Caroline Ball
Designed by Eric Drewery
Illustrations by Nicola Gregory and Valerie Hill
Room plans by Amanda Patton

All rights reserved. No part of this book may be reproduced or transmitted in any material form
(including photocopying or storing it in any medium by electronic means and whether or not
transiently or incidentally to some other use of this publication) without the written permission of
the copyright owner, except in accordance with the provisions of the Copyright, Designs and
Patents Act 1988 or under the terms of a licence issued by the Copyright Licensing Agency,
90 Tottenham Court Road, London W1P 9HE. Applications for the copyright owner's written
permission to reproduce any part of this publication should be addressed to the publisher.

Distributed in the United States by Sterling Publishing Co., Inc.
387 Park Avenue South, New York, NY 10016-8810

British Library Cataloguing-in-Publication Data
A catalogue record for this book is available from the British Library

ISBN 0-7063-7779-6

Printed and bound in Spain by Bookprint S. L., Barcelona

CONTENTS

INTRODUCTION

'Every design decision is an opportunity, not a problem!' – not an easy dictate to follow when your house is in chaos, your partner is asking for the umpteenth time when it will all be over and when every item of clothing you own is covered in a thick layer of dust. However, if you can keep this phrase at the forefront of your thinking, decorating will once again become the pleasurable process it should be.

It is so easy to lose sight of the purpose of interior design and for the whole process to become a major worry. Will the new carpet wear well? Does it go with the sofa? How deep should the curtain pelmet be and what sort of lighting is needed in a dining room? Mistakes are likely to be expensive or at the very least embarrassing and, rather than failing, many people opt for a less-than-exciting choice or for making no decision at all.

It is with just such questions in mind that this book has been written and it is hoped that the contents will tempt even the most timid to 'jump in' and have a go. Perhaps the most comforting aspect is that very often there is no wrong or right way of doing things – just degrees of appropriateness, and so long as the results are pleasing to you, the decision can be deemed to have been successful.

I grew up in an age when interior design as a profession was in its infancy and the consensus seemed to be that it should be practised only by people with something called flair. True, a creative talent is of great benefit to the designer, but, just like riding a bicycle, design is a skill that can be learned and, with practice, performed successfully – with or without flair!

Style is an area of great debate and choosing one for your home can cause dreadful dilemmas. Ideally it should be formed from a combination of the innate style of the building and a reflection of your taste rather than from the current opinion of the interior design press or what a previous owner has thought fit.

The actual process of decorating can become a thoroughly enjoyable one too. Once the method of arriving at decisions has been simplified and the design process has been divided into 'bite-sized' portions which follow a logical pattern, the whole thing becomes more manageable and, with everything under control, it is possible to have the most enormous amount of fun.

Decorating is also a great adventure. No designer, however experienced, knows in advance precisely how a room will take to its new dressing – and there is always that tantalizing moment when the last few components are put into place before the exact result is known. Because no two rooms are entirely the same, even the professional designer is sometimes surprised by the results, and what works in one room may not in another. But experimentation is part of the thrill of decorating and few errors of judgement are beyond reprieve, often requiring little more than the juggling of furnishings or an additional coat of paint to put right.

Interior design is not important in the scheme of life. We can surely get by without it and there are unquestionably much weightier subjects to involve us. Yet it can be the source of immeasurable pleasure and satisfies that very vital force of nest building that is in all of us.

Enjoy!

THE DESIGNER'S APPROACH

Space

One of the questions a professional designer is most often asked is: 'Just where do I start?' Without a doubt, you start here – with the space. It is not until you have organized the structure enclosing the space that you can begin to decide upon the wallpapers, fabrics and furnishings.

What makes many of us shy away from rethinking the structure is probably a combination of the regard in which we hold what someone else has deemed appropriate, a fear of the irreversibility of structural changes – and cost. But when you purchase a new house, there is little chance that your lifestyle or household coincides with that of the previous owners. Much better, then, to divert a portion of the decorating budget towards adapting the structure to meet your needs and devote rather less towards decoration and furnishings which can always be built up gradually in the years to come. Although not possible in every case, it is a great idea to live in a new home for some months before finalizing any decisions on radical changes. In that time you will experience the house's shortcomings and can judge just what you can and cannot live with.

There are many reasons why you might want to change the structure of your house in some way:

▶ **Change of lifestyle** You may need to make office space at home, or want more room to entertain.
▶ **Additions to the household** The arrival of a new baby may make you consider building an extension.
▶ **Lack of character** The addition of a fireplace or even simply a cornice may make a room more interesting.
▶ **Insufficient natural light** A larger window might make a dark corridor more inviting.

The problem may require major surgery or could possibly be solved by doing something as simple as rehanging a door on the opposite axis.

It is just so tempting to dive in and start looking at fabrics and paint charts before any of the planning has taken place – I even know of some professionals who simply can't resist the temptation to finger fabric samples at the mere mention of a new commission – but it really does pay dividends to do things the right way around. When designers are planning a project, they follow a very specific sequence: they examine and change, if necessary, the **structure**. Then they plan the arrangement of the **furniture**. That done, they plan the **lighting**. Finally, they select the **scheme**.

Each operation logically follows on from the completion of the previous one: you can't plan the lighting before you know where the furniture is going to be sited and it would be quite illogical to choose upholstery textiles when you are not sure how many seats your room will accommodate.

Drawing up room plans is where most designers start; this allows them to explore the possibilities of the space and to come to terms with its limitations. Professional plans tend to look highly technical, but are just a way of communicating ideas in a graphic medium. In other words, they don't have to be works of art so long as they say what you want to say. With a simple but accurate plan you can indicate to your builder any structural amendments you wish to make, calculate where to place items of furniture and work out an ideal lighting plan. The comforting fact is that it is extremely easy to learn how to draw simple room plans – and, after the first one, they get very much easier!

ROOM PLANS MADE EASY

1 Draw a rough sketch of the outline of the room. Try mentally to strip the room of all its embellishments and concentrate on the structure itself.

2 Measure the lengths of all walls, projections and recesses and then mark these on your drawing. To double-check the measurements, add together the lengths of each feature and see if they equate to the total wall length.

3 Make a note of such details as width and position of windows, swing of doors and room orientation (north, south, east or west).

4 It is also useful to make a record of any services (gas point, radiators, plumbing, light switches and so on), architectural features (such as dado, sloping ceiling, arch, floor level changes) and existing finishes (type, material, colour and condition).

5 Now, using the measurements from your rough sketch, draw up an accurate room plan to scale. The easiest way to do this is on graph paper with 2 cm squares (each of which will represent 1 metre of your room) divided into smaller squares of 2 mm (each equalling 10 cm of your measurements). Based on these calculations, your finished room plan will be one-fiftieth of the actual size of your room and so should happily fit on a sheet of A4 paper.

6 On the finished to-scale outline add the positions of radiators and other services, the ceiling height measurement and an arrow to indicate north.

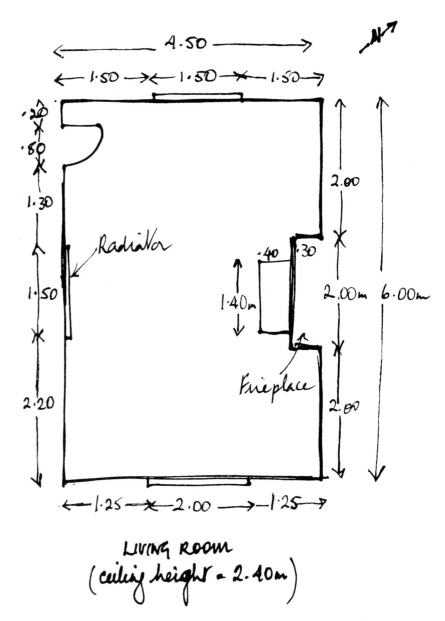

Rough sketch for room plan, with measurements noted.

MAKING THE BEST OF A ROOM

Now that you have a graphic record of the size and shape of your room, any problems that exist will be shown up. You can then decide how the room's appearance can be improved and the best way to make it a more convenient space to live in.

It is very helpful at this stage if you take a good hard look at the room: what are its qualities – a classic cornice, a stunning period fireplace or perhaps a beautifully shaped window? Make a note of these. Now do the same for any unattractive characteristics. Is the ceiling too low? Do

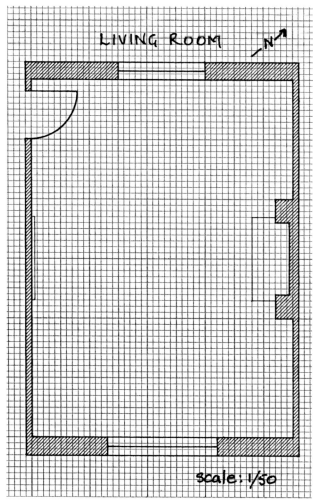

The same room as a finished scale plan (here shown reduced), drawn up on graph paper.

- Mirrors can visually double the size of a room. Sheet mirror above a fireplace can be a cheap alternative to a framed one. Ensure the verticals coincide with the uprights of the fire surround, not the mantel shelf ends.

- In an asymmetrical room, box out wall recesses to match existing features (these can form useful storage areas too).

- To ease the flow of human traffic and to get the best view on entering a room, it is preferable for the door to swing back against a wall rather than into the room space.

- Bring a disused fireplace back to life to give a room character and form a focal point. Where no fireplace exists, a false chimney breast can be built and a fire surround attached.

- Make an aesthetically inconvenient door 'disappear' by converting it into a jib door – that is, by treating it in exactly the same way as the adjacent walls, skirting/base board and all.

- To give a bathroom a less clinical look, install a concealed built-in cistern to the WC. The disguise can be completed by placing a commode chair over the pan.

If you are proposing to make any major structural changes, it is important to consult a professional (architect/surveyor/builder) to ensure that your ideas are feasible, within building regulations and safe to undertake.

CHANGING SPACE VISUALLY

The apparent size and shape of a room can also be vastly improved by less physical means (and, incidentally, by ways that don't cause so much damage to the pocket). The clever choice of surface texture – glossy if you want an area to appear larger, for example – and colours – pale and cool for a feeling of space – can visually change the dimensions of your room. Similarly, pattern can alter the proportions of a room, and lighting can be used to draw attention to, or away from, a feature. But first, let us consider the difference the choice and arrangement of furniture can make.

you need more space for the activities you have planned? Is the window too near a corner? The two lists will provide you with a starting point, enabling you to decide what to highlight and what to change or disguise. Here are a few problem-solving ideas:

- A cupboard door opening out into a limited area can be split and made into double doors so that, when opened, they take up half the space.

- Built-in cupboards can be disguised by treating their fronts (and sides, if any) in exactly the same way as the surrounding walls, continuing any architectural details (such as skirting boards and cornices) along their length and sides.

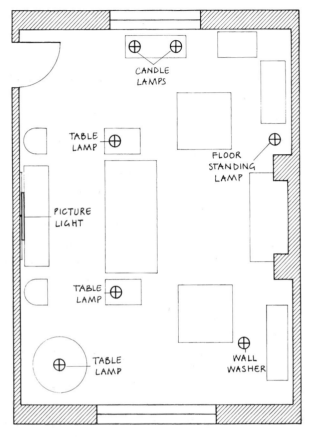

Using a room plan to work out the arrangement of furniture and lighting requirements.

ARRANGING THE FURNITURE

Have you ever ordered a sofa, only to get it home to discover that it swamped your room? It is a very easy mistake to make: relative to the large space of the store, the sofa would have seemed much smaller than it now appears. With your room plan, however, you will be able to place the sofa to scale on the drawing to gauge its impact before you make your purchase. Mistakes with furniture mainly occur through lack of planning, so think about what activities will take place in the room (for example, dining, watching television, letter writing, bathing), what furniture and storage each activity will require and how much space each function will take up. Consider also how human traffic will circulate through the room

Physically moving your furniture around the room can be a little tiring and, in any case, the furniture may not be to hand at the time. Instead, draw it to scale on your room plan. Stencils which feature common interior furnishings are available from most drawing office suppliers – remember to buy one that is compatible with the scale of your drawing. Alternatively, make card cutouts (also to scale) and move them around until you have a happy arrangement. Try to arrange furnishings so that people entering the room are greeted by a pleasant view.

One final thought: when ordering furniture, consider access to the house. Calculate just how various items can be moved into position (this may involve removal of a window or hiring a crane for cumbersome pieces).

Seven Secrets to Choosing Furniture

1 A three-seater sofa rarely accommodates three people happily. Instead consider ordering a three-seater made up with two seat cushions.

2 If you choose furnishings with colours that closely match their intended background, the items will effectively disappear, leaving a much less cluttered look. If you wish a piece of furniture to stand out, this effect can be achieved by choosing a contrasting colour.

3 In a small room, scaling down the size of furniture will not necessarily help, but using less of it will.

4 In a dining room, make sure you leave at least 75 cm/2½ ft of space around your table to allow for chairs in use.

5 In a kitchen, wall units that extend right up to the ceiling will eliminate an obvious dust trap and also provide extra long-term storage.

6 Stools and poufs are useful for occasional seating, take up little space and can sometimes incorporate storage space in their base.

7 Storage! Storage! Storage!

Lighting

For too long lighting has been treated as an accessory, an afterthought to pretty up a room once all the real business of designing has been completed. But with the range and sophistication of fittings now available, we should think of lighting as a wonderful tool that can bring our rooms to life. Not only can a well-planned lighting scheme make a room appear larger and more attractive but, more importantly, it will facilitate the various activities to be carried out there. It will help engender mood, too – drama for a dinner party, a restful ambience in a bedroom – and, with a little thought, assist in highlighting your room's best qualities.

PLANNING A LIGHTING SCHEME

A problem that frequently arises is when, long before the furniture is in place, we need to decide on the positions for sockets, points and switches. This dilemma can be resolved by resorting to your room plan on to which you have laid out your furniture. From this you will be able to see at a glance just where light will be needed and you can draw in the light fittings in the most appropriate positions. Nothing is more unpleasant to look at or as dangerous as an electric socket with multiple adaptors and cables trailing spaghetti-like across the floor, so it clearly pays to think ahead. Here are some points to bear in mind:

▶ Which type of lighting would be most appropriate for each activity? Is the storage associated with these activities well lit?

▶ How many fittings and what wattage will be required to achieve a good overall level of light?

▶ Is there a balance of light throughout the room, and have you made sure there are no dark areas?

▶ What is the general colour scheme to be? A predominantly dark, matt scheme may need more than double the total wattage of a pastel scheme or one with reflective surfaces.

▶ What is the ambience you want to achieve? Dramatic or reflective, workmanlike or seductive?

▶ What of future room changes? Do you have enough free-standing light fittings that can be repositioned to accommodate new functions?

Only after considering these points is it advisable to select the actual fittings.

SELECTING THE RIGHT FITTING

Before settling on a **style**, consider first the **performance** of a particular fitting rather than its decorative value. Will the light cast be of a suitable quality and will it fall in the right place?

Lighting has undergone a revolution in the past twenty years, and perhaps the most intimidating factor is the sheer quantity and variety of modern fittings on offer. To simplify matters, these can be roughly grouped as follows:

Downlighters

As their name suggests, downlighters direct a beam of light downwards, thus focusing attention on the lower part of the room (useful to distract attention from a too-high ceiling). The width of beam depends upon the bulb and reflector installed, so the one fitting can be made to perform in various ways. Downlighters may be surface-fixed (to ceiling, wall or track), semi-recessed (where there is limited space available above the ceiling) or fully recessed (preferable if you wish to 'lose' the fitting).

Wall Washers

A wall washer is, in essence, a downlighter that directs a beam of light to one side instead of straight down. When positioned in a ceiling approximately 1m/3ft away from an adjacent wall, an angled beam will flood that wall with light – perfect for lighting a large wall hanging or collection of pictures.

Uplighters

As you might imagine, these direct light upwards and are ideal for illuminating a decorative or beamed ceiling. A free-standing model, placed on the floor or on a table, can be used to cast a beam of light on an adjacent wall – useful when picture lights and wall washers are not a practical alternative.

Spotlights

The use of spotlights in homes has been somewhat superseded by more discreet fittings. However, they are still an excellent highlighting tool and, as they are highly directional, allow for changes to your room arrangement.

Low-voltage Fittings

With the voltage reduced by means of a transformer, these miniaturized fittings are highly favoured because they can fit into the smallest of spaces and can cast an extremely bright, tight and cool beam (excellent for highlighting displays). Although low-voltage lighting is economical to run, the necessity for transformers is likely to add to the initial cost. These need to be located near the fittings (some are even incorporated within the fitting) and should be sited for easy maintenance.

If all this sounds just too technical, do not despair. Armed with your room plan and furniture layout, plus details of any electrical installations, a good lighting shop should have no problem in recommending the most suitable fititngs.

At last, we can allow ourselves to think about the actual fittings for our scheme. They will form part of the overall design and therefore offer an opportunity to reaffirm your selected room style. Mixing modern fittings with more traditional styles presents no problem, as long as, in a traditional setting, modern fittings are as discreet as possible.

Let us first review the main categories of fittings.

Ceiling Lights

Although the ceiling pendant is still the most common source of overall lighting, the effect of the light given off can be rather deadening. To overcome this, attach a dimmer and rely instead on other more focused lighting (such as downlighters, spotlights and wall washers). To avoid glare from a ceiling fitting (especially in a low-ceilinged room), make sure the bulb is well recessed or shielded by a shade, 'lid' or baffle.

Wall Lights

These may take the form of traditional brackets, uplighters, downlighters, picture lights, striplights or

The effects of different light fittings (clockwise from top left): ceiling downlighter; picture light; table lamp with coolie shade; floor-standing uplighter.

angle-arm lamps, and can be chosen to throw light up, down or out.

There are various theories about the best height for wall fittings, but as a rule about eye-level is a good starting point.

When you are planning the position of your pictures, consider attaching a picture light to the frame of a painting (rather than to the wall) and running a cable behind the picture to a small wall socket. This will give you greater flexibility should you decide to substitute the picture for one of a different size.

Floor/Table Lamps

As these lights are not fixed to floor, wall or ceiling, they offer the greatest degree of flexibility. The traditional standard lamp has come of age – streamlined and weighted for stability, and some modern types are even height-adjustable: ideal for where there is no convenient table upon which to place a lamp.

Table lamps are an excellent source of decorative lighting, while at the same time introducing a soft pool of light. What better way to illuminate a group of objects or a gorgeous table-top flower arrangement?

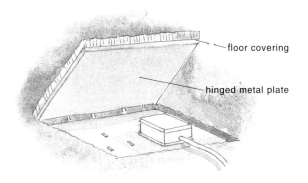

A floor socket, fitted flush and covered with a hinged plate – invisible when not in use.

SWITCHES AND SOCKETS

The ideal position for switches to all the lights in a room is at the entrance. This avoids the inconvenience of feeling your way in the dark to switch on individual lights. Equally, this arrangement simplifies switching everything off upon leaving the room. The average room may contain a number of different fittings, and by connecting these to several different circuits (switches) you will have the flexibility to illuminate just some or all of the lights at once.

The generally accepted height for a light switch is about 1.4m/4ft 6in, but you might like to consider placing the switch plate lower, at a height of about 90cm/3ft – nearer normal hand height and less intrusive, especially if it can be neatly tucked just above or below a dado rail.

Try to choose a style of switch plate to go with your scheme, or install an anonymous-looking clear acrylic one that will hide the workings but allow the wall finish to show through.

A dimmer switch will let you control the brightness of light – particularly apt for living rooms, dining rooms and bedrooms. The mood can be changed at the touch of a switch! Another useful device is a two-way switch, which allows you to switch a light on from one position and off from another. They are particularly suitable for corridors and stairways, and are a must for bedrooms (unless you enjoy leaping out of bed last thing at night!).

Always plan for more sockets than you currently need. Double sockets cost little more than single ones and in recent years our requirements have increased enormously – who knows what new gadgets we will be using next year? For free-standing lamps located in the centre of a room, a flush-fitted socket installed in the floor will avoid trailing cables.

To disguise socket plates, paint them to match your wall (use oil-based paint at least for the first coat). And to minimize their appearance, select plugs and cables that tone with the colours of your decor, rather than the standard bright white.

CHOOSING SHADES

Despite the huge range available, most lamp shades come in three main shapes: drum, empire and coolie, each dispersing the light in a different way. There is only one way to select the right size of shade for a table lamp, and that is to take the lamp base to the shop and try various combinations. The popular formula that the diameter of the bottom of the shade should be equal to the height of the lamp base is not reliable; so much depends upon the shape of both.

The positioning of a shade on a lamp base is determined by the shade 'carrier'. This metal framework may be part of the structure of the shade or bought separately (they are available in various heights). It should hold the shade so that, when viewed from eye level, all of the lamp base is visible but the metal working parts above are concealed.

Finally, before you buy, be sure to view the shade with a light inside it – shade colours and materials have an immense effect on the quality of light given off.

Bulbs

▶ Although they come in dozens of different styles, bulbs have two main types of fitting caps: ES (Edison screw) and bayonet.

▶ The variety of tints now available is useful for giving a warm glow to a room or to 'cool down' its colours.

▶ Bulbs for low-voltage fittings are expensive but last much longer.

▶ Touching a bulb (especially one for low-voltage fittings) with your bare hands tends to reduce its life span – use a cloth or tissue when installing.

▶ Use fluorescents sparingly – although ideal for work areas (providing economical, shadow-free light), they are prone to distort colours and are likely to give a chilly feel to a room.

Colour, Pattern and Texture

COLOUR

All decorators have a magic wand in their tool box. It can evoke a particular period or mood; change the apparent proportions and size of a room; lighten a dark room and impose harmony through a house. This magic tool is called colour and clearly it would be foolish to ignore such a wonderful device!

Every day of our lives we are influenced by colour – manufacturers and advertisers do not arrive at certain colour choices on a whim. In the same way, in your home you can learn how to use colour to create exactly the room you desire. However, let us first look at the 'grammar' of colour, illustrated by the colour wheel opposite.

Red, blue and yellow are primary colours (denoted by '1'), so called because they cannot be made from a combination of any other colours. Secondary colours ('2' on the wheel) are formed by combining their primary neighbours on either side – so for instance, orange is produced by mixing red and yellow. All other colours are gradations between these segments.

The wheel also divides into 'cool' and 'warm' halves, although those near the dividing line can veer either way – egg-yolk yellow would be thought of as warm, while greenish-yellow has a cool effect. If you wish to open out a space and make it appear larger, choose colours from the cool side of the spectrum, as these tend to 'recede' visually; equally, a large area will seem smaller and more intimate if decorated in a warm colour that 'advances'.

Selecting Appropriate Colours

Paint manufacturers, in an effort to assist and inspire homemakers, now produce an almost unlimited array of colours and our difficulty is in choosing from such an enormous range. Opting for magnolia in every room is many people's (and many a builder's) way of playing safe, but it also means missing out on so many wonderful opportunities. To narrow down your choice of colours to a reasonable number, ask yourself these questions:

What is the orientation of the room? A room facing north may benefit by being in a colour from the warm side of the spectrum.

Do the proportions of the room need some help? Painting a low ceiling in a light colour will make it appear higher.

How much time will you spend in the room? A very vibrant colour may be wearing in a room where you pass a lot of time.

What is the period/style of the room? 'Heritage' colours, available in many ranges, will add authenticity to a period style or theme.

What mood do you wish to create? Is the living room, for example, to be lively or tranquil?

When will the room be used most? Light quality can render colours very differently. If a room is used mainly at night, make sure that your selection looks good in artificial light.

Which existing possessions do you wish to accommodate in the room? Their colours may inspire the starting point for your scheme.

Let's suppose your living room is rather small but has a relatively high ceiling. The room is north-facing and has an existing brick-coloured carpet. Your considerations might be:

- a light wall colour to expand the space;
- a warm colour to counteract the northern light;
- to take the colour over the ceiling in a slightly darker shade to bring down its height.

A pale shade of terracotta might just be the answer.

Colour can be used very effectively to link different areas in a home. A hallway carpet in yellow, beige and tan, for example, would provide the opportunity to develop schemes based on these colours in the rooms leading off the hall – one room in yellow, perhaps teamed with blue; another in tan, possibly combined with cream and brown.

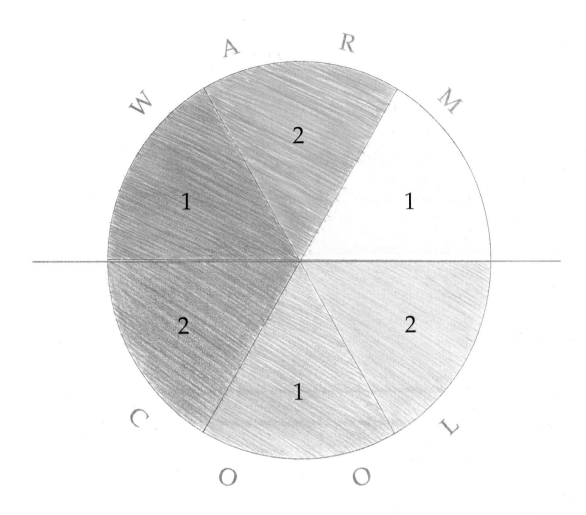

Four Main Types of Scheme

The Neutral Scheme relies on such 'non' colours as white, grey, brown, beige and cream. It is the perfect foil for interesting accessories, paintings and so on, and creates a mood of calm sophistication – ideal for a formal drawing room.

The Monochromatic Scheme is based upon just one colour. Far from being boring, the subtle variations of tone and shade and reliance on textures can be both soothing and full of interest. It would be an admirable choice for a bedroom.

The Harmonious Scheme is composed of colours that fall within one half of the spectrum – for instance, blues and greens, pinks and violets, yellows and oranges. The lack of violent contrasts makes these decorative schemes restful and easy to live with.

The Complementary or Contrast Scheme uses colours that lie on opposite sides of the colour wheel – green with red, blue with orange. It creates a vibrant, lively scheme – great for young people and for rooms that are perhaps not used for long periods at a time. The contrast makes each colour seem more intense and, for the association to work well, it is preferable for one colour to dominate.

Ten Tips on Using Paint

Paint is a most wonderful medium – it's simple to apply, comes in any number of shades and finishes, is not vastly expensive and can be manipulated in many ways. Best of all, if you make an error over the choice of colour, you can simply paint over with another hue.

1   When choosing from swatches, go for a colour that appears slightly lighter and less strong than you want. When covering the walls of a room, it reflects upon itself and intensifies.

2   Tinting your own colours can be great fun. Simply buy either white paint or the colour nearest the one you want and add tints until you achieve the exact shade you desire. Remember always to mix sufficient for your purposes as it will be almost impossible to repeat the recipe.

3   Beware of magnolia! In some lights it has a yellow tinge, in others an inclination towards pink. This may be an effect you enjoy – if not, select another colour.

4   Should you require an exact match to an item of furnishing, some paint shops will custom-mix paint of this colour.

5   In an older property brilliant white tends to look too modern and clinical. Choose an off-white shade that will give the effect of aged white paint.

6   On woodwork, consider a softer satin or eggshell finish instead of gloss.

7   Before painting an entire room, try a test area and check how it looks by day and by night, on a sunny day and on a dull one.

8   If replacing ceramic wall tiles is beyond your budget, consider painting them. First apply a coat of PVC adhesive diluted 1:1 with water. When dry, this will form a key on to which an oil-based paint can be applied. If you want to add painted decorations, such as stencils, finish the tiles with a coat of clear polyurethane varnish for protection.

9   If your newly painted walls look too bright, too light or too dark, adjust the colour by sponging over the surface with the original colour into which a little white or black tint has been added. Not only will this help to correct the colour, but it will also give an interesting textured effect.

10 Remember that paint always dries to look a little darker than when wet.

Being Bold with Patterns

When using several patterns in one room, you will find that they work best when linked – perhaps with colours, themes, motifs or textures in common. Two dominant patterns of the same scale will tend to 'fight' each other for your attention, so go for patterns of varying scales. Start by choosing one main large pattern, then find medium- and small-scale ones to complement this and fill in with plains. Always view patterns from the distance at which they will be seen, and remember that small patterns will merge and appear plain from some way away.

Related patterns of different scale working well together.

PATTERN

Design schemes are often referred to as colour schemes, but there are two other ingredients that are every bit as important as colour. It is by skilful use of pattern and texture that a scheme will be brought to life and given an extra dimension.

Designers of wallpapers, fabrics and carpets spend endless time perfecting colour and pattern combinations, so why not tap into their skills and take your lead from the colours that they have deemed go together well? Try assembling samples of materials that pick out the individual colours featured in your chosen patterned fabric and you will be surprised how quick and easy it is to muster a scheme.

To make several differently coloured existing possessions appear to 'belong' together, find a patterned fabric that includes the colours of the furnishings you already have – you will find that they will be drawn together by the colour links.

When selecting a patterned curtain fabric, it is a good idea to obtain a large sample and drape this in folds – you will be surprised how this gathering process can distort patterns – usually in an acceptable way, but not always. View curtain fabric samples with the light *behind* them rather than in front, to check how the material will appear when hung in place at a window.

TEXTURE

With the growing trend to pare everything down to a minimum, an even greater reliance is being placed on interesting textures. It is possible to spend hours carefully selecting and putting together colours and patterns, but this won't ensure a successful scheme if insufficient attention has been given to textural quality. A totally 'flat' scheme of materials with similar finishes will lack life and seem dull. By juxtaposing contrasting textures you will create excitement – just think of a coffee table with a polished marble top on a floor covered with rough matting, or lustrous chintz cushions on a matt flannel sofa.

Texture can also have a big influence on how colour is perceived: a matt material such as velvet fabric or emulsion paint will absorb light, rendering it darker, while a shiny surface will reflect it and make the colour appear brighter and more intense.

To test the part that texture plays, try making up a scheme using plain fabrics of only one colour – say, cream. Find as many differently textured samples as you can and you will be amazed at what an interesting scheme you can compose.

To get good value from your selected textures, focused lighting is imperative. To see how true this is, take a powerful torch and point it at different furnishings within your home. Notice how the beam of light brings out the textural quality and gives objects a three-dimensional 'moulded' effect – that is what you are after.

Pattern-on-pattern works well so long as each is of a different scale, as the soft furnishing on this sofa suggest. Colours and motifs link the individual patterns.

Assembling a Scheme

Having considered the various elements that go into a scheme, it's time to think how these can be assembled into a pleasing whole. In fact, most of us practise putting together schemes nearly every day of our lives . . . when we get dressed! We choose a style that is appropriate for the activities we intend carrying out, we select materials that are suitable and colours that flatter us. Formulating a decorative scheme for your home is very much the same process.

A good starting point, if you lack inspiration, would be to create your own style file. Begin a collection of any pictures of interiors or furnishing details from magazines that particularly appeal to you, and you will soon see your style preferences emerging. Another starting point could be your existing possessions. The combination of colours in a favourite painting or a rug might inspire a scheme. Lacking these, you might like to seek out an interestingly patterned carpet or fabric to set

you on your way. The idea that professional decorators always have a clean sheet to start with is a fallacy.

Each room scheme should work well with its neighbouring areas. That is not to say that the schemes must all be very similar, but rather that they should have some linking factor. For instance, a dominant colour from one room might be used as an accent colour in the next. Hallways, stairs and landings in fairly neutral colours will allow you to merge easily into any variety of stronger colours in the rooms that lead off them. In a smaller property, laying the same carpet throughout tends to lend a greater sense of space and unity and, as a bonus, is often cheaper than buying small quantities of differing colours.

Skilled at visualizing though professional designers might be, they still need to see how all the components of a scheme interact, and the best way to do this is to make a sample board.

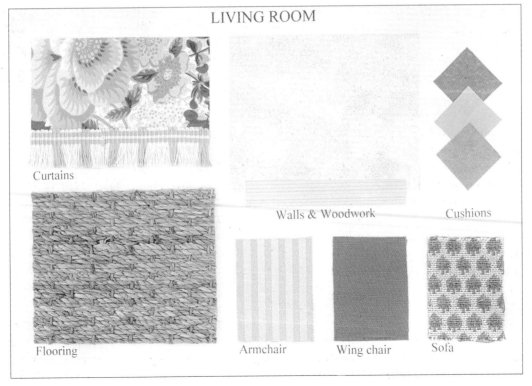

A sample board.

Most stores and manufacturers are willing to provide small cuttings of fabrics, wallpapers and carpets without charge. For a large-patterned fabric that is pivotal to your scheme, a larger sample will better demonstrate how the material will look when made up. Many suppliers will provide a returnable length, or it may be preferable to buy one for testing purposes rather than having the material made up only to realize your mistake. Collect more samples than you need, to see how different effects work together.

Always view samples in the room where they will be used and on the plane on which they will appear – stick wallpaper samples to the wall with masking tape, lay carpet samples on the floor and try out paint on a board that can be held up to the walls. Fabric can take on a very different appearance depending on whether it is laid flat or gathered into drapes.

When you are building a scheme around existing furnishings, you will need colour samples of these, too. Where no off-cuts exist, colours from paint charts or strands of wool might be used as a colour reference instead. Keep the samples for each room together in a clear plastic file.

When you have collected your samples, you can make a sample board.

A SAMPLE BOARD

Artist's A2 mounting board (about 45×60 cm/1ft 6in×2ft), or any neutral-coloured board, forms an ideal base for your display of samples. Simply attach them to the board – double-sided tape is the easiest method – and label each one with its purpose.

Just as room plans need to be a true representation of the room in miniature, a sample board needs to reflect the mix and balance of colours and materials in a scheme. Try to position the samples according to their location in the room (carpet at the bottom of the board, wall and curtain samples near the top) and if possible relate the size of the sample to the area it will cover in the room – your wall covering sample should be larger than your cushion fabric sample, for instance. If it helps you to visualize the finished room, include any other items that will form part of the scheme, such as illustrations of light fittings and furniture.

When your board is complete, you will be quite surprised how well it represents the way the colour-

mix, the textural contrasts and array of patterns will work in the finished room. Any anomalies or imbalance should show up now, and if your scheme is too dark or too bland, or has too many patterns, this can be corrected at this early, inexpensive stage.

A SCHEME SHEET

As a back-up to your sample board, or when there is insufficient time to prepare a board, you can make up a scheme sheet. This is a mini sample board and has the advantage of fitting neatly into a file.

The scheme sheet consists of an A4-size form (easily drawn up by hand or on a personal computer), with three columns. In the left-hand column list each surface you are going to decorate (walls, sofa etc.). In the centre column write any information you consider relevant to describe the finish or material you will use. With small samples (say, 3 cm/1½ in squares) attached to the last column, the sheet can be slipped into a clear plastic sleeve and carried with you on your next shopping trip.

ROOM-BY-ROOM DECORATING

LIVING ROOMS

Just where do you start with the decoration of a living room? With so many activities to cater for and so many people to keep happy, this room will be successful only if planned meticulously. A good living room is one that on a practical level happily accommodates the various activities you wish to undertake in the space while at the same time being aesthetically pleasing in its role as a reception area.

Your starting point is, as always, to determine exactly what you want from your room as this will dictate how you will arrange the space. Is it to be:

▶ **a leisure room** for quiet reading, listening to music, letter writing, watching television?

▶ **a dining room** for family meals, smart dinner parties, television suppers?

▶ **an entertainment room** for family parties, video viewing, card games?

▶ **a hobbies room** for dressmaking, model making, arranging a stamp collection and so on?

▶ **a work room** for study, wordprocessing, homework, research?

▶ **a mix** of all or any of the above?

These various activities all require specialized lighting, ample storage facilities and suitable furniture. By listing them you will help to focus your mind on what is needed.

When it comes to planning a furniture arrangement, it is important to establish a focal point in your room – a point of interest that can be highlighted and around which furnishings can be gathered. In a living room the most obvious focal point is a fireplace, but if one does not exist another point of interest will need to be selected: perhaps the room has a handsome window with an attractive view beyond, an important piece of furniture, a collection of paintings or even an antique rug. In a very large or 'double' living room you may have several subsidiary focal points around which you will arrange 'conversation' groupings. If a television set has to be accommodated, this too will form a focal point and will have an influence on how the room is arranged.

Selecting a style for your living room should be an easy matter if you live in a period property as the theme may well be suggested by the style of architecture. In a more anonymous modern space you have the choice of imposing a traditional style by the addition of architectural details and furnishings of your selected period or of interpreting a contemporary and perhaps foreign idiom. Your scheme may be inspired by an existing possession – the design of an oriental rug, the style of a distinguished piece of furniture or even the colours in a favourite large painting.

A novel idea, popular in Victorian times and which you might think of reviving, is to change the look of your room with the seasons. Come spring, chair slip-covers, cushions, curtains and upholstery drapes can all be replaced with lighter fabrics to suggest sunnier times. A floral theme can be introduced by painting or stamping designs on to cheap plain canvas using fabric dyes. This material can then be used for a table cloth, chair slip-covers or even curtains. You might also think of adjusting your seating arrangement so that a garden rather than a fireplace becomes the focal point in summer months.

A beautifully flowered needlework rug provides the inspiration for a pink, green and cream colour scheme in this elegant drawing room.

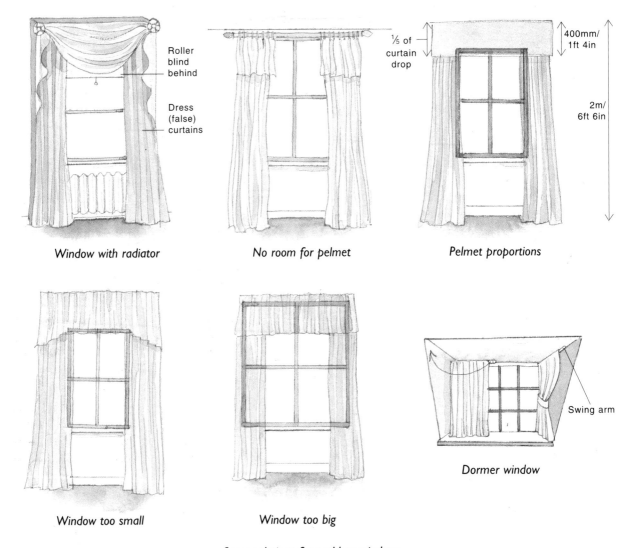

Roller
blind
behind

Dress
(false)
curtains

Window with radiator

⅕ of
curtain
drop

No room for pelmet

400mm/
1ft 4in

2m/
6ft 6in

Pelmet proportions

Window too small

Window too big

Swing arm

Dormer window

Some solutions for problem windows.

The usually generous windows to be found in a living room offer a great opportunity for decorative treatments, but always check first whether there is a style available that will improve the proportions of your window.

SURFACES

For many the starting point of a scheme is the flooring as this is where the largest portion of the budget is likely to be spent. Investing in a good-quality carpet or other floor covering will pay dividends as this is the item that will probably outlive many a different scheme over the years. When visiting a carpet show-room, look at the samples in their correct position – that is, horizontally on the floor – and, if possible, borrow a sample to view *in situ* in your home. A carpet with a mix of 80 per cent wool and 20 per cent synthetic material is generally considered ideal from a practical viewpoint, and the use of a good-quality underlay will vastly increase the life of a carpet as well as giving it a more luxurious feel. The suitability of wall surfaces will depend upon the use to which your living room is put. Whatever your choice, the inclusion of a dado bearing a more durable surface, such as paint or vinyl wallpaper, will help to protect the wall from damage.

FURNISHINGS

A single sofa or pair of sofas might be the centrepiece of your seating arrangement. The three-piece suite forms a traditional grouping, but as an alternative consider placing a sofa with two unrelated French bergères or add a wing chair and arm chair to give your room an informal air. This arrangement is particularly suited to the 'country house' look where a matching suite is an anathema. A three-seat sofa offers comfort for two people, but rarely for three. To avoid the inconvenient positioning of seat cushion joins when two people are seated, ask your upholsterer to make up the three-seat size with just two seat and back cushions. Something easily forgotten is that, if you propose to entertain a certain number of people to a meal, the same number of guests will also require seats in your drawing room. Additional seating, to be drawn up when guests arrive, might be provided by upright chairs against the walls and run-up stools slotted under a spacious coffee table. When selecting a curtain fabric, remember to view a large sample draped as it would appear when made up and with the light behind the material (again, as it would appear when at the window).

STORAGE

A vital ingredient of any successful living room scheme, storage cannot be ignored. If insufficient facilities are provided, all the expense and effort that went into achieving a good-looking living room is wasted if the room is constantly littered with books, newspapers, records, tapes, games and so on. Storage can be in either custom-made built-in units or free-standing items of furniture such as sideboards, bookcases, shelving units and desks. It should be planned at the start of your project and not just introduced as an afterthought. The recesses to either side of a chimney breast provide a useful space for building in cupboards with display shelves above, and a window seat that has space for storage within its base offers another solution and has the additional benefit of providing extra seating. Should this be your choice, do remember to select a window treatment to accommodate the seat. A combination of window blinds (festoon, Roman or roller) and 'dress' curtains should fit the bill.

LIGHTING

Nowadays living rooms have to accommodate so very many activities that providing suitable lighting for each of them can present quite a challenge. Hobbies, eating, watching television, reading, entertaining and relaxing quietly all require very different lighting effects and, in order to satisfy all of them, it is necessary to build in a fairly flexible system that can be adjusted as required. Free-standing fittings such as standard lamps, floor-standing uplighters and table lamps all provide for an easily changed arrangement, and having the fittings on several different (say, three) circuits will allow the opportunity to change effects easily.

The living room is also where you are likely to want to display your most treasured possessions. Be they valuable antiques or family memorabilia, they will all take on much greater 'value' when drenched in light. Pictures can be suitably lit by picture lights or overhead wall washers; collections displayed on a table top can be bathed in light from a downlighter or table lamp. A very successful method of lighting attractive book spines within a bookcase is to install discreet strip lights under or at the side of the shelves, always ensuring that naked bulbs are hidden from view, behind baffles where necessary. Glass shelves within a niche, lit from above or below by a downlighter/uplighter, will give you a wonderful opportunity to display your favourite objects.

Many people are reluctant to part with a central ceiling light, even though this is known to flatten surfaces and kill atmosphere. The reluctance is understandable in view of the attractiveness of some fittings (particularly chandeliers) and the good general light value they provide. So why not keep the fitting, but apply a dimmer to the controls? In this way you retain the decorative value of the fitting and the possibility of using the light for background lighting.

The recommendation to have several light circuits, switched from the doorway, is particularly apposite for the living room. As for the number of fittings to include, this is a difficult question to answer without full information on a specific room, but as a general guide for a mid-sized living room around ten fittings might be considered appropriate.

Formal Drawing Room

Most people's favourite room when it comes to decorating, a formal drawing room provides the most wonderful opportunity to demonstrate your decorating skills and to express your personality.

In all the other rooms discussed a preoccupation with the practicalities usually has to dominate, sometimes at the expense of aesthetic considerations. Although it has to perform and respond to our needs, the formal drawing room is above all a room for pleasure – to satisfy all the senses. This may involve some subterfuge where there is a conflict between what is needed for comfort and what appeals visually. Here are some examples:

▶ A television set cannot be anything but an ugly piece of equipment, yet hidden beneath a round table with a full-length cloth it need not be an eyesore.

▶ Radiators are rarely attractive, but can be disguised if encased in a box or painted to match their surroundings.

▶ Ugly contours in a room shape can be boxed in to give symmetry and provide storage.

▶ A badly proportioned window can have its dimensions hidden behind well-designed curtains (see page 20).

The style of a drawing room is most likely to be dictated by the period or style of the building that houses it; occasionally, however, it can be interesting to go against the architecture and so create drama by a clashing of the centuries. Antiques in a modern warehouse space or contemporary furnishings in a classical Georgian interior are just two examples of the excitement that you can create. Mixing periods within the same room is also a possibility, but needs to be done with skill. The most successful results are produced by combining contrasts: rough aged wood with smooth tubular steel; antique matt velvet with glossy chintz; polished marble with rough medieval matting.

This is a room where many people choose to display their most precious possessions – portraits of ancestors, family silver, collections – and it is important to bear this in mind when deciding upon a scheme. It is all too easy to go overboard and cover every surface with pattern, only to find that when accessories are placed they disappear against a dominant background. To avoid this an experienced designer will always gather together the accessories right at the start (or, if they are not yet accumulated, will have them in mind) and will think of them as part of the overall scheme. If you like your furniture, accessories and guests to star, select plain surface treatments and create a 'blank canvas' backdrop for your features.

Should flowers be your passion, leave space for a judiciously placed vase, and when planning flower arrangements, always take into consideration their surroundings – give thought to their colour and form within the context of your scheme. Try mixing fresh blooms with artificial greenery to make your bouquets go further and have in reserve further silk imitations for when fresh flowers are not to hand. If no flowers are available, try sprinkling flower essences in your room – you will find your guests searching for the bouquet.

When arranging furniture in a drawing room, view the room from every direction before settling on a format. Make sure that from each position you have a pleasant vista. The view of the room you get upon first entering is particularly important and sometimes this can be much improved by rehanging the entrance door on the opposite axis, so that it opens flat against an adjacent wall and you are able to view the whole room immediately.

Pretty pastels and modern furnishings contrast with traditional architecture in this light and airy drawing room.

HOW THE ROOM MIGHT LOOK

THE PLAN

This large room with its pleasing proportions provides an elegant space for a modern formal drawing room. The area is divided, courtesy of the furnishings, into two separate conversation areas, which has the effect of giving balance to the room and making a large space seem more intimate. This is primarily a receiving and entertaining room and so does not have to cater for other activities associated with family living. Storage (to house audio equipment and so on) is minimal in order to maintain a look that is uncluttered.

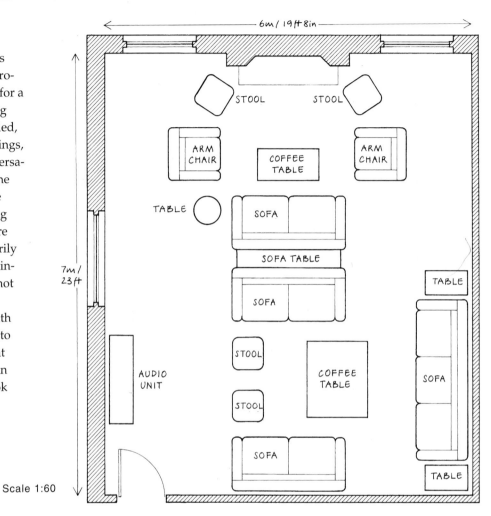

Scale 1:60

DESIGN DECISIONS

1 **Scheme** This exercise in pastels was inspired by the large abstract paintings.

2 **Polished wood floor** Practical and elegant, this reflects any natural light coming into the room, thereby increasing the feeling of airiness.

3 **White area rugs** These contribute to the lightness of the room and help to define the conversation areas.

4 **Sofa table** Minimal in width, this table between the backs of two sofas provides a useful surface for placing flowers and lighting.

5 **Mirror-faced coffee table** This adds to the light and airy feeling in the room and, although large, the mirrored surface helps it to disappear into its surroundings.

6 **Two double-cushion stools** While taking up very little room, these stools provide extra seating for visitors.

7 **Window treatment** Deliberately understated, the curtains allow the contours of the arches and the wrought-iron work beyond to speak for themselves.

8 Lighting Picture lights have been eschewed in favour of discreet, modern, recessed wall washers to highlight the pictures, while more traditional fittings have been included in the scheme to provide a welcoming ambience.

9 Accent Touches of black found in the smaller picture, the two vases, the garment hanging on the larger painting and the fireplace, provide a contrast to the pastels and give the scheme some definition.

10 Accessories Few, well chosen and all linking in some way with their surroundings, these are kept to a minimum so as not to destroy the purity of the room.

11 Flowers These well thought-out arrangements co-ordinate with the scheme and add a sculptural quality to the room.

Open-plan Family Living Room

For many people deciding whether or not to join two or more small rooms to create one large living space presents a major dilemma. Historically, and particularly in Victorian times and in the early twentieth century, many houses were built with a room at the front for entertaining and receiving guests and another separate one to the rear for family use. This arrangement no doubt suited life in the nineteenth century, but now our need is for more flexible living areas and for larger multi-purpose spaces.

You may wish to set aside areas for study, play, cooking, dining or perhaps a library, while at the same time still retaining the facility to open up these areas to form a larger space when required. Opening one room into another often makes sense, but before you forge ahead, remember that there is more to think about than just the size of the new space you are creating. What about noise, smells and untidiness – are you prepared for people using one area to be exposed to these elements from another?

For maximum flexibility and comfort build in plenty of storage so that toys, files and dishes can be quickly removed, install an efficient ventilation system to remove odours, and plan on plenty of soft surfaces to absorb sound. You may also wish to exclude children and pets from certain areas and these might require a barrier of some kind.

Once you have made the decision to join two or more rooms, it is necessary to think about just how much communal living will suit you. It is possible to go the whole hog and open up the spaces permanently (depending upon structural limitations), or you may wish to retain some form of separation to be put in place occasionally when required. A permanent solution might involve the use of an arch, a squared-off opening or even the complete removal of any traces of a dividing wall between two areas. Whatever your choice, do remember that this newly formed room is part of a larger architectural structure. Be careful not to create an imbalance in the distribution of space within your home as a whole and take care to continue any architectural theme already in place. This may mean installing columns at either side of an opening in a classical interior or perhaps fixing decorative corbels to an arch in a Victorian home.

Should you wish to retain the ability to shut one room off temporarily from another, there are various methods that can be employed. Doors (double, sliding or concertina) can be hung at the opening, a folding screen placed at the dividing line, a piece of furniture strategically located or curtains/blinds hung between the two rooms. If the quality of light in one room depends upon a

The colours of blue and terracotta combine happily in this open-plan family living area that invites you in and encourages you to relax.

window in the other, you might also like to consider glazed doors that will allow the light to be shared between the two spaces.

It is important that the vista from one room through to another be a pleasant one, so avoid placing furniture with its back facing an adjoining room. If you must position a sofa thus, place a sofa table at its rear to enhance the view. Ensure also that your passageway between the two rooms is unhindered. Flexibility will need to be built into any furniture arrangement and lighting scheme so that when you wish to use the rooms as a single unit, this can be done with a minimum amount of effort. A proportion

of free-standing lighting and furniture on castors will do much to help.

It is vital that the decorations in these individual spaces, that have now become one, act together harmoniously and that there is a strong sense of unity between the areas. This doesn't mean that the schemes have to match exactly, but they should relate to one another. For instance, a fitted carpet might be installed in a sitting area while a patterned area rug incorporating some of the carpet colours might sit on a wooden floor enclosing a linked dining area. Window treatments of the same fabric and similar style will also aid a feeling of cohesion.

How the room might look

THE PLAN

Three distinct areas are opened up to form a comfortable living space where the whole family can commune. The division between the kitchen and dining room is defined by a row of units that runs across the 'border' and which contain tableware – handy for table laying opposite. The sitting area is separated off by a tall cupboard that opens into the dining area. Another large storage unit (is it possible to have too many?) nestles neatly next to the chimney breast and houses books, audio equipment and a television.

DESIGN DECISIONS

1 **Scheme** Neutral colours and natural surfaces dominate in this easy-to-live-with, all-purpose scheme. Blue highlights provide a good contrast to the terracotta flooring and introduce a feeling of country freshness.

2 **Flooring** Sealed terracotta tiles provide a tough, easily maintained flooring that reinforces the country feel of this open-plan living area. An oriental-design rug links the blue of the sofa with the tan of the flooring

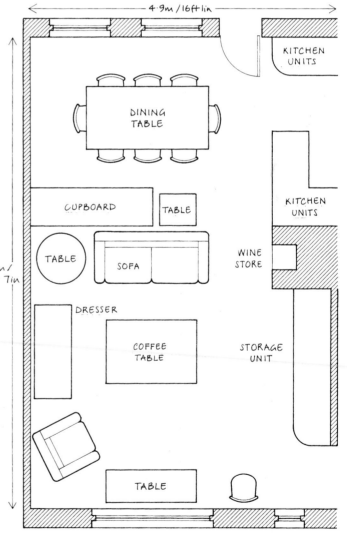

Scale 1:60

and brickwork. This also serves to soften and define the seating area.

3 Kitchen units The blond wood of these units is followed through into the other areas, being reflected in the finish of the dining table, tall cupboard, coffee table and storage unit.

4 Lighting Eyeball spotlights in the ceiling critically direct light where needed. Although the bulbs show, these are unlikely to cause glare because of the height of the ceiling. A traditional pendant light over the dining table provides plentiful light in that area and underscores the period feel of the room.

5 Sofa Foam-filled sofa seat cushions ensure that the sofa will take plenty of abuse and still remain in good shape. The patterned fabric cover discourages marks from showing. If this were treated with a sealant, removing dirt would be a matter of merely wiping over with a damp cloth.

6 Soft furnishings The off-white fabric chosen for the window and door treatments blends well with the walls and so does not conflict with the many architectural details (beams, leaded windows and so on).

7 Blue highlights The blue of the tiles and decorative plates in the kitchen reflects the sofa upholstery colour, thus helping to link the areas.

8 Accessories Kept to a minimum, these give a clean uncluttered look while at the same time suggesting a relaxed country air.

9 Wine storage This is provided by a group of clay pipes cunningly placed within a chimney. A strategically positioned downlighter turns this storage problem into a design feature.

In contrast to its city-centre location, this Gothic-inspired Chelsea conservatory introduces more than a hint of country elegance.

Conservatory Living

Can you imagine the joy of spending late autumn afternoons warmly lounging in the midst of your garden, of growing and harvesting your very own tropical fruits and of twilight summer suppers that are guaranteed rainproof? No, this is not a description of life on a faraway tropical island, but a glimpse of the pleasure to be had when you own a conservatory.

Yet another inspired Victorian concept that we are revisiting and appreciating anew, despite the disparity of lifestyles between then and now. A conservatory gives life a new dimension. It allows us to enjoy a garden year-round and stretches the living areas of our homes. All age groups can benefit: it provides an ideal space for a toddler to play in (the semi-outdoor finishes should stand up well), for an elderly person to relax in out of season, and for people of any age to enjoy atmospheric dinner parties.

Should you be on the brink of deciding to construct a conservatory, be sure to pin down your ideas well in advance:

▶ How much do you want to spend? A finished conservatory may cost more than you imagine and such extras as heating, lighting, wall and floor finishes, furnishings and plants can add considerably to an initial estimate.

▶ How will the finished conservatory look from outside? Do you wish its style to reflect the architecture of your home?

▶ Which direction do you wish your conservatory to face? A southerly orientated conservatory will be full of sunshine, but unless a good ventilation system is installed and shade provided (by blinds or by painting the glass), it is likely to overheat in summer. A north-facing glass house will receive little sunshine and so will require an efficient heating system for cooler days.

▶ To what purpose will you put your conservatory? Is it to be a place for indoor gardening, relaxing, dining, cooking or playing?

▶ Do you wish your conservatory to become an integral part of an interior living area and/or to open up to and become one with your garden or terrace? The larger your opening on to either or both of these areas, the more linked they will appear. Double, sliding or folding-back doors will help to achieve the connection you desire.

Because the conservatory represents a link between the house and its exterior, the most appropriate furnishings will be those that reflect this connection. Well-designed garden furniture, softened with table cloths, cushions and upholstered seats, will help to blur the line between inside and out, as will rattan, wicker or cane furniture. A floor of flagstones, scrubbed wood planking or terracotta tiles will underscore the connection. Accessories can provide a similar link – garden statuary, urns, plants and terracotta pots are all particularly suitable. The best window treatments are ones that do not detract from the view or interior planting. Tailored blinds or curtains of muslin or calico in a simple style are ideal.

When it comes to selecting a colour scheme for your conservatory, the choice is yours – but do remember that the exterior views will become your 'wallpaper' and indoor plants your 'accessories', so choose colours that blend well.

Lighting a conservatory is a relatively easy process so long as electrical points have been well positioned and there are sufficient sockets for free-standing fittings. Wall- or ceiling-mounted lanterns will look good, as will discreet spotlights focused on features. A well-lit garden will form a magnificent backdrop at night and a dining table might be lit by a simple country-style chandelier or candles in glass hurricane lamps on the table. Free-standing uplighters placed behind plants will add some magic to the room.

HOW THE ROOM MIGHT LOOK

THE PLAN

Despite space limitations and its modern construction, this upper floor of a two-storey conservatory in central London manages to create a feeling of airiness and tradition. A three-seat sofa and wing chair provide seating in this all-purpose living-space-cum-studio. A coffee table and round side table are provided for the convenience of the occupants and a large antique chest offers generous storage space.

DESIGN DECISIONS

1 **Scheme** Cool cream and green form the basis of this deliberately simple, fresh, rural scheme. The designer's use of country-style fabrics and natural materials are entirely apt in this 'back-to-nature' space.

2 **Conservatory style** The gracefully arched, glazed sections are mirrored in the contours of the railings outside the conservatory to give the room an air of elegance. A panelling detail to the lower part of the walls and doors adds interest.

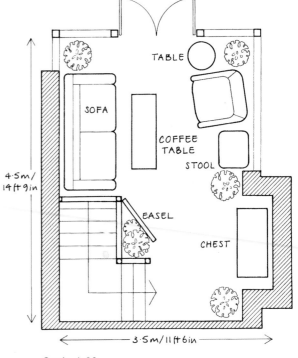

Scale 1:60

3 Walls Washed with palest cream to provide a perfect background for botanical prints, a choice of colour that encourages a feeling of spaciousness.

4 Flooring Sisal matting contributes a strong textural quality to the scheme and provides a robust floor covering for this indoor/outdoor surface.

5 Upholstery A deep and comfortable three-seat sofa encourages leisurely relaxation, and a profusion of cushions with check and zoological-patterned covers shows up well on the dark green striped cover fabric. On the opposite side a plaid-covered wing chair is draped with a length of green checked fabric to soften the chair outline.

6 Blinds Operated by a system of cords on cleats, cream-coloured fabric blinds continue the unified look and keep the sun's rays from damaging furnishings and overheating the room.

7 Lighting Table lamps and a naive metal chandelier were chosen to reflect the traditional styling of this conservatory and to give it a homely air.

8 Door furniture Fine details are the hallmark of the professional designer. Here, handsome brass bolts, handle and hinges lift the whole scheme and give it a quality finish.

9 Planting The variegated greens of the foliage blend well with the overall scheme and help to link inside with outside.

KITCHENS

The kitchen has taken on a much more strategic role in modern times. Once purely an 'engineering' room, it is now more often regarded as the social centre of the home. In line with its new function a typical modern kitchen is more likely to be decorated in an altogether warmer, homelier style. Gone are all traces of laboratory lighting and outhouse floorings and in their stead have come a wealth of living-room attributes.

This does not mean to say that the primary purpose of a kitchen – cooking – can now be ignored. Food preparation must of course be at the forefront of any design decision made for this very important room. One of the most difficult rooms to organize (mistakes will irritate on a daily basis), it requires loads of common sense and forethought to eliminate wasted energy and to make the room a pleasure in which to work and play.

If you are starting from scratch, choosing the right-sized room for your kitchen can be critical. Too small a room and you will have difficulty in accommodating all that you require. Too big and the preparation of each meal will involve you in a marathon. Sometimes the use of two inter-connecting rooms can provide the best answer, the main one being reserved for cooking and the secondary

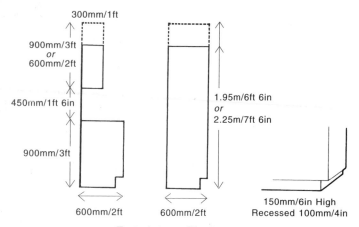

Typical sizes of kitchen units.

Hi-tech metal shelving sporting beautifully arranged kitchen paraphernalia and hardwood units provide all the decoration needed in this serious cook's kitchen.

34

one for food storage, laundry, dining or other activity.

It is always a good idea to start by listing all the activities you wish to cater for in your kitchen. Apart from the obvious ones related to cooking, you may wish to launder and iron clothes, arrange flowers, serve informal meals, store party equipment, accommodate a central-heating boiler, provide space for a child to play and so on. If your kitchen has a door to the exterior, you may also need to allocate space for the storage of outdoor clothing, and if there are pets in the house, finding them a corner in which to curl up may be a priority. When you have completed your list, it's time to draw up another detailing all the equipment and storage requirements necessitated by the various activities you have listed.

Having established exactly what is required in the way of equipment, workspace and storage, the easiest way to determine the best position for everything is to draw up a scaled plan of the room (see pages 5–7), remembering to mark in the positions of windows, doors and service points as these will have a strong influence on the location of major items. Then, using tracing paper over your plan, you can try out different arrangements, always starting with the most important items – the sink, cooker and refrigerator. When you have finished, it is advisable to track the movements around your kitchen that might be involved in preparing, serving and clearing away a typical meal. Can any of these journeys be avoided by switching the positions of any items of equipment?

Easily forgotten is the matter of waste disposal. A small skip might be appropriate in some kitchens, but a more practical solution may be the combination of large swing-bin (preferably housed within a unit) and a waste disposal unit attached to the sink. A waste compactor will also help minimize the volume of waste for disposal. Ventilation is another aspect easily overlooked: do you really want to be reminded of what you ate for dinner last night?

There are various solutions – a vent in a window or exterior wall or an extractor system over a hob that recycles the air through filters. Best of all, however, is an extractor that wafts kitchen vapours directly to the exterior.

Once all the important planning decisions have been made, it's time to decide upon the style you wish to adopt. Perusal of kitchen magazines and brochures plus visits to showrooms should fill you with inspiration.

SURFACES

Paint is probably the most suitable wall finish in a kitchen, but this doesn't have to be boring old flat cream. Choose from any number of decorative finishes – stipple, rag or other broken surface. Conjure up a country-kitchen feel by the use of stencils or create your own faux finish to complement your kitchen units. Wallpaper, so long as it is washable and is well adhered, can also be used.

Surprisingly in a kitchen the floor, being a relatively uninterrupted surface, often offers the best opportunity for a design statement. First fashionable in the 1960s and 1970s, cork is probably one of the most appropriate floorings. It is quiet, soft underfoot, doesn't readily show dirt and is easily cleaned. A vinyl woodstrip flooring (vinyl with a thin veneer of natural wood) performs as well as any synthetic floor but has the advantage of having a natural look. Cushioned vinyl floorings are popular and old-fashioned linoleum is enjoying a revival. All these floorings can be cut to your own design in any number of shades or have a contrasting border incorporated. Other hard finishes such as quarry tiles, flagstones and ceramic tiles are all suitably durable, but may be noisy and a little tiring on a busy cook's feet.

The most common finish for worktops is laminate. A much-improved product, this is now

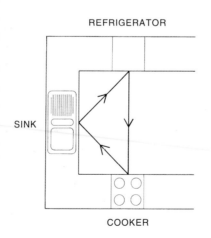

REFRIGERATOR

SINK

COOKER

The working triangle.
For convenience your passage
between these three main elements
should ideally form a small triangle.

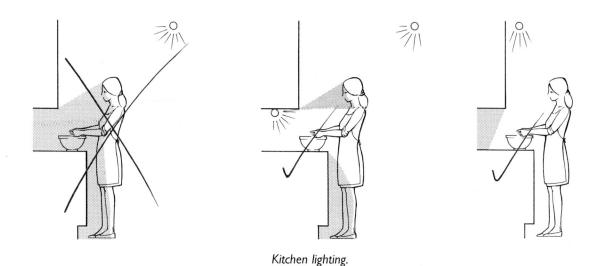

Kitchen lighting.

able to stand up well against hot pans and sharp knives. It looks particularly smart with a deep, post-formed, rounded edge. As an alternative, various types of stone (granite, slate, marble and so on) can give a touch of luxury. To save on cost and weight, these surfaces can be relatively thin, with a double depth at the edge to fool the eye into believing that a greater thickness has been used. Wood is a wonderful material and makes an attractive top for a country kitchen. Tiled tops have found favour, but are difficult to keep clean and care should be taken to avoid germs being harboured within the grouting.

FURNISHINGS

Furnishings are best kept to a minimum so as not to hinder movement around the kitchen. Tall stools (with a seat height of about 70cm/27in) are suitable for under a standard worktop and provide for spontaneous meals or a rest for the tired cook. It is advisable, for both aesthetic and acoustic reasons, to introduce some soft finishes into this otherwise rather hard-edged room. Padded seat covers for the seating and your choice of a textile window treatment will help. Curtains are not always the answer – the window recess may be shallow and curtains might dangle inconveniently over the worktop surfaces – and blinds generally prove to be a more acceptable solution. Whatever your choice, all fabrics should be washable.

STORAGE

Frequency of use should be a strong determining factor when planning storage. High and low levels are best left for rarely used items, while eye-level spaces should be reserved for items that are used every day. In many instances a ceiling can provide useful extra storage space. A rack can be fixed from which can be suspended any number of objects (preferably items that are both practical and at the same time decorative).

LIGHTING

As with all good planning, practical considerations come first. In this case the preparation of meals must be top of the list. The mistake most frequently made is not in the selection of fittings but the siting of light sources. It is vital that light beams are cast exactly where you want them and that they are not interrupted by shadow. To ensure this the light source must come from directly above the work surface rather than behind the person working at that position. Avoid spotlights on a centrally positioned track as almost inevitably this will mean you are working in your own shadow. Instead consider ceiling-fixed downlighters over your work surfaces or strip lights fixed to the underside of wall units and shielded from view by baffles.

To create a more social atmosphere in dining/relaxing areas of the kitchen it is advisable to have at least one other circuit of lighting which can be switched on when food preparation is completed and the lighting over work areas is extinguished. A rise-and-fall pendant fitting over the dining table provides a most suitable light, as does a downlighter. And for those special occasions, nothing beats the intimacy and cosiness of candles. Additional soft lighting around the room could come from a combination of table lamps and wall lights.

Cook's Kitchen

The kitchen takes on so many roles in modern times that it is sometimes easy to lose sight of its primary purpose. The starting point when planning a kitchen for the dedicated cook has to be the equipment. Whereas many kitchens may have only a basic oven or microwave, the true cook will undoubtedly be seeking altogether more specialized appliances.

Cooking, it should be remembered, is a physically tiring process and everything possible should be done to minimize unnecessary work, travel around the kitchen and wear and tear on the cook. The layout of the working cook's kitchen is unlikely to have units simply ringing the room. A central island or 'peninsular' unit is a most important factor in the reduction of kitchen traffic. A mobile unit on castors is also a useful addition to kitchen furnishings.

In the serious cook's kitchen, storage may well be without doors and open to the elements – quick and easy access being an obvious priority. To ensure that the vast array of exposed equipment and worktop space is kept impeccably clean and does not become covered with a fine film of grease resulting from the cooking vapours, a heavy-duty ventilation system is essential. When planning your storage requirements, do not forget to allow a slot for cooking manuals.

The surfaces within the well-used kitchen will be chosen for their robustness and ease of maintenance. Stainless steel is a favourite work surface and, as well as being tough, easy to clean and hygienic, it can look

Everything in this clean-cut kitchen, with its many serviceable surfaces, shouts 'We mean business.'

extremely smart in a modern setting. A bright idea for the busy cook is to set a cutting board into the worktop as a permanent fixture – so much easier than having to seek out a loose one from within a cupboard.

For walls and ceilings, a paint finish that will stand up well in humid conditions (seek individual manufacturers' advice) is likely to be your first choice. Dark colours are rarely seen in a kitchen but, with the right artificial lighting, can provide a stunning background to complement your food. The area between wall and base units is generally faced with ceramic tiles – a good finish that can also provide an opportunity for decoration.

Any floorings discussed in the general introduction (see page 36) would be suitable for this busy kitchen, but do take care that the surface beneath the floor covering is well prepared in the first place. Any faults in the underfloor will soon show through and with time the flooring will wear unevenly.

When we think of a chef's kitchen, the most likely image is of a very modern, streamlined room devoid of any decoration or charm. But there really is no reason why a country kitchen (see page 46), centred around an old-fashioned range, should not serve the same purpose so long as certain essentials are in place: namely, good working appliances, plenty of clear work surfaces and masses of accessible storage.

For ideas on how to equip your kitchen, visits to the showrooms of catering kitchen manufacturers can provide inspiration. Here you will see a vast array of equipment and appliances rarely displayed in a domestic supplier's showroom and you can seek out advice from the professionals.

HOW THE ROOM MIGHT LOOK

THE PLAN

The island unit in the centre of this working kitchen provides a useful extra work surface as well as somewhere to serve informal meals. Its positioning also means that cooker, refrigerator and sink are never more than a few steps away from the working/serving area. Notice how the sink has been located in front of the window so as to provide maximum natural light and a view, and the cooker is positioned so that vented smells can easily be trunked to the exterior.

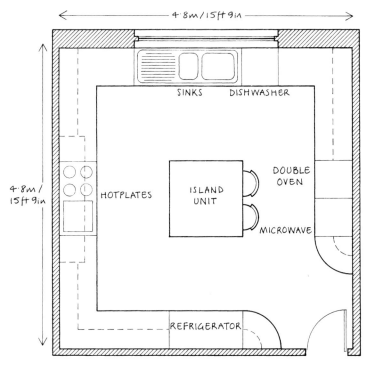

Scale 1:60

DESIGN DECISIONS

1   **Scheme** More about materials than colours, this simple scheme centres attention on blond wood, stainless steel, marble and brick.

2   **Flooring** Wood planks provide a warm, easily cleaned, hard surface perfectly in keeping with the use of natural materials in this kitchen.

3   **Island unit** A convenience for both the cook and the diner, this unit, with its handsomely proportioned top, allows plenty of overhang to ensure room for seating comfort. An inset section made from the same marble as the worktop elsewhere in the kitchen is convenient for chopping, pastry-making and laying down a hot pan. A channel around the perimeter catches any loose liquid. The brick of the unit base adds a contrasting texture to the smooth stainless steel and polished wood.

4   **Stools** Two in number and sleek of design, these allow the busy cook to rest or to enjoy an informal meal in company. When not in use, they slot neatly beneath the worktop.

5   **Sink** One-and-a-half sinks are surrounded by a stainless-steel top and have a useful swing-arm mixer tap. A waste disposal unit beneath the half-sink ensures that kitchen garbage is kept to a minimum.

6   **Cooker hood** Faced with stainless steel and of serious proportions, this hood ensures that cooking odours linger less.

7   **Window treatment** Venetian blinds provide a no-nonsense window treatment that is neat, practical and continues the hard-edge look.

8 Lighting Pendant space-age fittings located over the island unit and sink are well targeted and their sculptural quality reinforces this kitchen's modern theme. Pin-hole downlighters, discreetly recessed into the ceiling, lift the overall level of lighting.

9 Metal racks To either side of the cooker hood, these make use of 'dead' space and provide long-term storage for pans and other cooking utensils.

10 Wine rack This stylish criss-cross unit not only stores bottles but also provides a design feature in this aesthetically and ergonomically planned kitchen.

11 Wall clock An essential ingredient for the time-conscious cook.

City Kitchen

For some the preparation of meals is a task to be reduced to a minimum. This might be from choice, priority time being given to work commitments, study or social activities outside the home, or it may be caused by the simple lack of space. Whatever the reason, to cater for your needs it will be necessary to refine your kitchen operations and equipment in a minimal kitchen.

While the best space in an apartment is likely to be devoted to reception rooms and bedrooms, the kitchen is frequently relegated to the remaining area. This might be under a staircase, in a corridor, off a hallway or in some small internal room. Having decided on where the kitchen is to be sited, the next matter for your attention is whether to have the kitchen exposed or cleverly concealed from view. Cupboard doors, a screen or blinds can all be used to good effect in this regard.

Overcoming lack of space and natural light are likely to be the biggest problems faced in a small kitchen. However, much can be done with careful selections:

► Pale, cool, reflective surfaces will visually enlarge the space, as will the use of similar colours for all surfaces – details can be added in contrast to give interest.

► Space can also be saved by swapping a conventional door at the entrance to the kitchen for one that takes up less space. This might involve a sliding door, double doors (which open in half the space) or concertina doors.

► Clean lines and constant levels help to give a kitchen a streamlined appearance, as will the installation of an unfussy window treatment (Venetian, roller and Roman blinds are particularly suitable).

► Artificial lighting can be used to advantage. Plan on providing a good balance of light in your kitchen – any areas remaining in shadow will visually disappear, thus making the room appear smaller. Ceiling-fixed recessed down-lighters and strip lights fixed to the base of wall units will provide excellent lighting conditions. Should your kitchen have a disproportionately high ceiling, this can be disguised to some extent by concentrating light in the lower portion of the room.

► The effect of placing mirror tiles on the wall between the base units and upper units is most impressive. They add glitz, increase any natural light and visually open up the space.

► It may be tempting to go for reduced-sized appliances (as supplied for boats, caravans and so on), but select full-size equipment if you possibly can. This will allow you a greater variety of items to choose from and, should you later move on to a larger space, your equipment will be reusable.

► The microwave cooker has revolutionized our lives and is particularly suitable for the small city kitchen. Not only does it take up a much smaller space than a conventional oven, but it also simplifies the cooking process.

► To enlarge your worktop space, incorporate pull-out extending surfaces that slot under a normal worktop.

To increase storage space, build in extra-high wall units. The upper portion of these can be used for longer-term storage and fold-up steps for reaching can be kept nearby. Extra storage can also be eked out of the wall space between the upper and lower units if a racking system or cup hooks are installed. In a tall kitchen the ceiling space could also be brought into use as a storage area with cooking utensils hung from hooks suspended from the ceiling.

Walls of high-gloss Devonshire cream and an arrangement of classical busts give nothing away in this hallway kitchen of a London apartment.

HOW THE ROOM MIGHT LOOK

THE PLAN

Sculptures in this entrance hall kitchen take their inspiration from the exhibits in the Soane Museum in London and help to disguise the room's rather surprising dual role. Cupboards to either side of the desk open up to reveal a far more domestic purpose than first appearance might indicate.

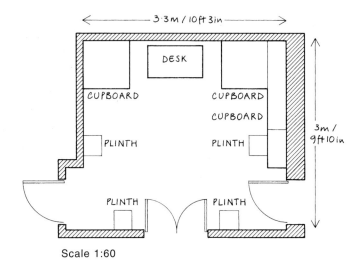

Scale 1:60

DESIGN DECISIONS

1 **Scheme** Glossy walls of pale yellow enlarge the space and create a soft background upon which classical busts are displayed.

2 **Flooring** Coir matting provides textural interest and a robust finish suitable for this 'traffic' area.

3 **Desk** A shelf pulls out from the underside of the Victorian standing desk to provide a useful work surface.

4 **Cupboards** Flanking the desk, these are built in and finished in the same way as the walls so that they appear to be part of the structure. Note how the cornice and skirting/base board has been continued across the cupboard fronts and sides so as to complete the illusion.

5 **Lighting** Strongly focused downlighters highlight the wall-hung plaster busts, while wall-fixed swing-arm lamps illuminate the desk. The cupboards open to reveal additional downlighters to light the contents.

AN ALTERNATIVE KITCHEN

THE PLAN

Squeezed into 'dead' space on a landing with stairs leading off, this narrow kitchen is both decorative and functional. The units are full depth and cleverly accommodate all that the minimal cook might require. Fitted against one wall, this slender kitchen takes full advantage of the airy space above the stairs.

DESIGN DECISIONS

Scheme Whatever the season, this spring-like scheme, with its sponged pale yellow walls and jade units highlighted with white, will always feel fresh and bright.

Flooring Practical pale green linoleum tiles are bordered by a darker green to give the area definition.

Units Chosen for their decorative quality, these Gothic-inspired units are painted in a delicate shade of green.

This smart landing kitchen, with its elegant units and pretty colours, does not need to be concealed.

Shelves Filled with decorative objects, these help to give the kitchen a less than utilitarian look.

Lighting Four eyeball spots focus on the kitchen worktop and on pictures on the wall opposite. Additional working light is provided by strip lights under the wall units.

Pictures Positioned high up on either side of the prettily arched window, the two paintings ensure a pleasant view from the kitchen.

Plants Artificial foliage suspended from the ceiling to conceal an air vent continues the country theme.

Country Kitchen

What a wonderful picture the term country kitchen conjures up: visions of flowers drying over an Aga cooker, dogs curled up in a corner, home-made orchard-fruit preserves in pots on a rustic dresser, freshly gathered garden-grown vegetables in a basket and the smell of newly baked bread permeating the whole house. The room reeks of tradition, wholesome food, country values and a sense of permanence, summing up an altogether more tranquil approach to life – an attitude that seems ever more desirable in times of pressure, insecurity and rapid change.

Of course, such a kitchen style is best suited to a house or cottage set in a rural location, but this does not preclude it from being adopted in a more urban situation. The urban kitchen might open out into a conservatory rather than a picturesque cottage garden and a cat might replace the hunting dogs, but there is no reason why the essential elements of country style should not be embraced in the city.

The essence of country-kitchen style is that everything should look as though it has had a chequered past. This is best demonstrated by including old items that have in fact been used over generations – perhaps bought at country auctions, purchased from antique shops or haggled over at car-boot sales. Newly constructed articles, manufactured to modern standards and 'distressed' to give an instant feeling of age, can also be incorporated. These may well have the advantage of offering a better performance while still evoking times gone by. A gas-, oil- or electrically-powered range will suggest a bygone age without requiring stoking, and modern units behind doors of aged wood will be easier to keep clean and will not warp.

Units are best when they appear to have evolved rather than having been installed all at the same time and from a matching suite. Although it is preferable for the carcasses to be modern, the facings can be manufactured from aged timber and, for the correct look, should be free-standing rather than in a continuous run. A central wooden table and a large ceramic Belfast sink with wooden drainer and old-style taps will help to reinforce the style.

Surfaces within the country kitchen are most likely to be natural or at least natural-looking. Wood dominates and can be used for units, worktops, flooring and even walling. Flagstone floors are traditional and terracotta tiles will give a similar country feel to a kitchen. Painted wall surfaces are in order and nature's rich colours – leaf green, earthy terracotta, sunny buttercup yellow and gentian blue – provide a perfect background to complement all that timber.

This is one kitchen style for which curtains might be the preferred choice of window treatment. Unpretentious materials such as cotton gingham, ticking, butter muslin and calico make a strong rural statement when used for simply gathered country-style curtains.

The most suitable lighting arrangement here would be to combine high technology with simple country-style fittings. The modern fittings should be discreet and provide a good working light (recessed downlighters and/or strip lights behind baffles are a suggestion), and traditional wall lights, table lamps and old-fashioned overhead pendant fittings will help to set the mood.

Although we tend to think of the country kitchen as being essentially English, there is no reason why you should not create your own Portuguese, American, Mexican, Italian, Moroccan or other ethnic kitchen. What fun could be had in collecting implements, crockery and other cooking kit in foreign lands and finding ceramic wall tiles, cupboards and floorings from far-away places.

Cream and buttermilk combine with blue to offer a warm welcome in this fresh country kitchen.

HOW THE ROOM MIGHT LOOK

THE PLAN

A country-style dining table forms the centrepiece to this spacious, traditional kitchen. The Aga cooker on the right nestles neatly in the chimney and units to either side house pans, baking tins and so on. On the opposite wall a dresser, laden with china, provides additional storage space. The 'sink with a view' makes full use of natural light in its position under the window and a dishwasher is accommodated nearby. Double entrance doors are flanked to one side by a refrigerator and on the other by a tall cupboard. The door on the right leads to a butler's pantry and that on the left to a dining room.

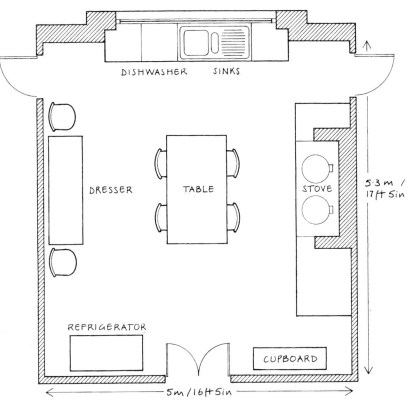

Scale 1:60

DESIGN DECISIONS

1 **Scheme** Fresh creams bring sunshine into this north-facing kitchen and blue china plates 'paper' the walls to provide interest and contrast. A blue border neatly contains the wall space to give the room a tailored appearance. A dado of wooden boarding reinforces the country feeling and continues the worktop line.

2 **Flooring** A natural-coloured hard floor surface is practical, especially in cooking and washing up areas, while a cotton rug brings softness to the dining area. The colours of its stripes help to bring the scheme together.

3 **Units** Panelled doors and simple brass knobs give these units a country feel and the cream-painted fronts help them to disappear into the wall surface.

4 **Work surfaces** Slabs of hard-wearing granite provide a touch of luxury. Notice how it is also used for the splash-back around the sink and how it forms a useful shelf behind the range.

5 **Furniture** A country-style table and chairs provide a suitable setting for informal meals. Wooden seats are softened by tie-on cushions with blue-checked covers.

6 Window treatment The lack of a soft finish to these windows is no loss when handsome architraves are on display. A border of blue completes the treatment.

7 Lighting Modern technology and traditional fittings combine for an apt lighting arrangement. The charming old-style wall lantern is electrified and the Victorian-fashion pendant fitting over the dining table has a rise-and-fall mechanism to allow height adjustments.

8 Shelf Formed from a length of cornice, the shelf above the Aga provides a surface for display and has under it a pole for drying kitchen cloths.

9 Accessories Great control has been exercised in the selection of accessories. Their common blue colour helps to give this kitchen a sense of unity and order.

DINING ROOMS

Unlike our Victorian ancestors who believed in each room in the home having a specific purpose, today we tend to think of dining as a movable feast to be undertaken wherever most convenient or wherever the television is located.

It is not so long ago that the dining room was considered very much the heart of the home and few houses were constructed without one. It was where families assembled on a daily basis and where all important festivals and rites of passage were celebrated. But times have changed and in most modern homes the kitchen has in many respects supplanted the dining room as the family gathering room. The dearth of house servants to transport and serve meals, the hectic and conflicting timetables of family members and the general lack of space have all rendered the dedicated dining room, for many, a disposable luxury.

However, the kitchen can provide a most excellent space for dining. Generally the warmest room in the house (an important factor in cooler climes), it allows food to be served directly from the preparation area and also enables the person preparing the food to enjoy the company of others fully as the meal is processed.

Other areas you might consider for a dining role are a portion of a living room, a hallway, a study or even a conservatory. It makes little sense to deprive a child of his/her own bedroom, a spouse of his/her study or guests an overnight stay in order to preserve a room that otherwise might be used only for occasional entertaining. But there is no reason why a room cannot serve two functions. With cleverly chosen lighting, the selection of dual-purpose furnishings and inventive use of storage, a room might provide a space for several purposes most successfully.

If you are in the happy position of being able to reserve a room specifically for dining, how do you go about selecting a space within your home? It goes without saying that for convenience this needs to be sited in close proximity to where the food is prepared. Our ancestors may have found tepid tea and lukewarm lunches acceptable when houses were larger and servants plentiful, but today's busy lifestyles yield little time for scuttling along corridors and space is not easily given up for that piece of furniture appropriately known as a dumb waiter. Hatchways through to the kitchen, once much favoured, are currently rather less fashionable and are being replaced by open-plan kitchen/dining rooms. The size of room is obviously a factor for consideration, as is the view from the window if the room is to be used primarily during daylight hours.

When deciding upon a style for a dining room, think carefully how it will marry up with your/your family's eating habits and your desires for entertaining. You need to ask yourself:

▶ What household members need to be accommodated (numbers and ages)?

▶ When will the room mostly be used – day or night time, summer or winter?

▶ How many people do you like to entertain at any one time?

▶ Do you prefer to entertain formally or informally?

▶ What mood do you wish to create?

Pleated raspberry fabric, with a gilt fillet edging, lines the walls of this colourful dining room lit by a Dutch-style chandelier with tall candles.

SURFACES

The treatment of surfaces will very much depend upon your style of dining. For a family they will naturally have to be fairly resilient to stand up to daily wear and tear. The floor merits special attention. This needs to withstand the scraping of chairs (take care with stretchable natural floorings and any that are not stable or well adhered to the floor itself). The acoustics of the room should not be ignored. Half a dozen small children dragging wooden chairs on a hard floor surface can be quite deafening, especially if there are few other soft surfaces in the room.

FURNISHINGS

The centrepiece of the room is naturally the dining table and much will depend upon your choice of the most suitable shape and size for your purposes. Many people favour a round table, which has the advantage of eliminating disputes as to who should sit at its head. It also allows conversation across the table to be enjoyed between all diners rather than only between those positioned adjacently as is the

case with a rectangular table. An additional benefit is that there is greater possibility for squeezing in an extra guest, especially if your table is a pedestal type (that is, one with a central pillar rather than legs around the perimeter). The table size is also critical: too small and it will not happily accommodate all your dishes, and diners will not be able to eat in comfort; too big and conversation will be difficult and traffic around the table may be hindered.

STORAGE

The main items requiring storage are likely to be table mats, napkins, silverware and glassware, and it is a great advantage to have these stored where they are easily to hand. A sideboard will provide conventional storage, but perhaps cupboards and shelves might be constructed within niches to either side of a chimney breast. The bulk of your items could be placed within the cupboard space, while the more decorative items (pretty china, glass and silverware, for example) could occupy the display shelves. An unused fireplace can

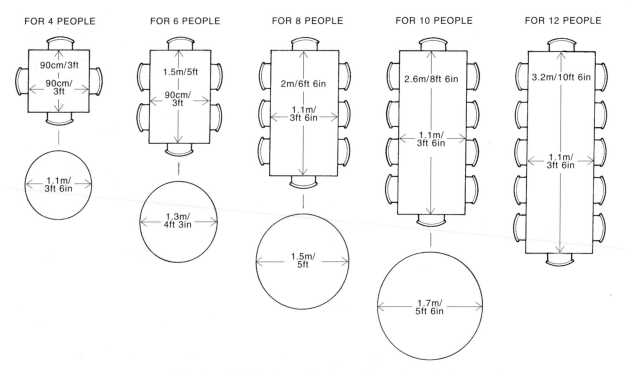

Table sizes for dining in comfort (approximate dimensions).

Bouquets of stencilled
flowers border the sloping
ceiling and carry the eye
upwards in this pretty
country setting primed
for breakfast.

provide useful storage for wine. Simply fill the space with clay pipes (see page 27) and store bottles on their sides within the pipes.

LIGHTING

Dining rooms probably offer the greatest opportunity for planning creative and dramatic lighting effects. As they are frequently used at night and for entertaining, a little theatricality is not misplaced. The star feature in any dining room will inevitably be the table and, of course, the diners – and flattery of both is your aim.

Traditionally the table would be lit by an overhead light fitting – frequently a chandelier type – which, although adding to the decorative value of the room, may not provide ideal lighting conditions or even a controllable source. To overcome the deadening effect of light cast from such a fitting, a dimmer could be attached to it and downlighters installed to provide more easily manipulated light sources.

The highlight of your table, apart from the dishes you serve, will no doubt be a centrepiece and, whether a humble bowl of fruit or an elaborate flower arrangement, this will benefit enormously from being swathed in light. A recessed low-voltage downlighter casting a narrow beam will highlight this beautifully. The addition of candles, be they in smart silver candlesticks or within a hurricane glass, will soften the effect and cast a pleasing glow on guests' complexions.

Of critical importance is that nothing should interfere with cross-table communications. Attention therefore needs to be paid not only to the height of any table decoration but also to the position of light fittings over the table. A rise-and-fall system attached to an overhead pendant light will allow you to adjust the height precisely, and candle sizes can be selected to ensure that they do not cause a distraction. A crown-silvered bulb will help to prevent glare in guests' eyes.

To complete your plan, softly focused lighting around the perimeter of the room will ensure that the table does not appear in a vacuum; it can also be useful in illuminating a serving area.

Get the lighting right, and at the flick of a switch your 'café' will turn into a sophisticated restaurant!

Dedicated Dining

A licence to entertain! Formal dining is surely all about theatre, drama – a performance. We are continually being told that the dinner party is dead and that, in modern life, a dining room is a luxury we can all live without. True, we can get by without one, we can invite friends for supper and entertain them in the kitchen surrounded by all the clobber of cooking, but anyone who possesses a room dedicated to the pleasures of eating and entertaining knows how much it adds to the richness of home life. For a few hours we can suspend reality and pretend that the world is a wonderful place where every sense is pampered and everyone is beautiful.

For a start it presents the most amazing opportunity for showing off – for bringing out grandmother's china service, for polishing the family silver, for decorating the dining table with exotic floral delights and for wearing the most glamorous of outfits. We all need to escape, especially after a hectic, distinctly unglamorous day.

The decoration of your dining room can be quite idiosyncratic – it is part of your theatre and the set you create will depend upon the tale you wish to relate. Think of all the restaurants you really admire and enjoy lingering in. Would the style of any of them translate well into your space? Is your taste for a sophisticated, cool, modern look? Or perhaps French rustic style? Write down half a dozen words that best describe your favourite look and use these as your starting point.

Choosing a colour scheme for a dedicated dining room can be great fun. Banished are the restraints that pertain to some of the other rooms in your home. There is no need to select a safe calm scheme here – the likelihood is that you will occupy the room for only relatively short periods and so can afford to go for a stronger statement than, for instance, in a bed-room or even in a living room. If your room will be used primarily at night, the problems associated with balancing natural light need no longer limit your choice. Colour psychologists will tell you that red stimulates the appetite (did the Victorians know something we claim to have recently discovered?) and it is certainly a colour to encourage animated conversation. Whatever your decision, it is vital to try out the colours/materials in the light in which they will be seen.

Lighting is probably the most important factor when it comes to setting the mood in a dining room. As your guests enter the room, a great theatrical trick is to limit the lighting to just one very strong narrow beam (preferably from a recessed downlighter) directed over the centre of the table where you have placed a most magnificent centrepiece. Even the humblest bowl of herbs, presented in this way, will take on altogether new dimensions of interest. As all the guests assemble, you can then switch on other lighting sources to continue with the meal.

When dressing the table, never think of its accessories in isolation. Whatever you put on the table in the way of centrepieces, cloths, mats, napkins, china, glassware and so on will instantly become part of your overall scheme, and each piece should be chosen with this in mind. It is therefore necessary to practise some restraint when selecting a scheme to ensure that, when all is in place, the two most important elements – your guests and your food – are complemented by and not in competition with your decorations.

Dressed to entertain: this traditionally styled dining room promises pleasure.

HOW THE ROOM MIGHT LOOK

THE PLAN

This fortunate space happily accommodates a dinner for ten with room to spare. The door on the left leads to the kitchen, while double doors open on to a hallway. A tall ceiling results in elegant proportions suitable for a grand treatment. Items of antique furniture fill the spaces to either side of the fireplace and a Regency sideboard occupies the wall opposite. Gilt console tables flank the double doors in this pleasingly symmetrical room.

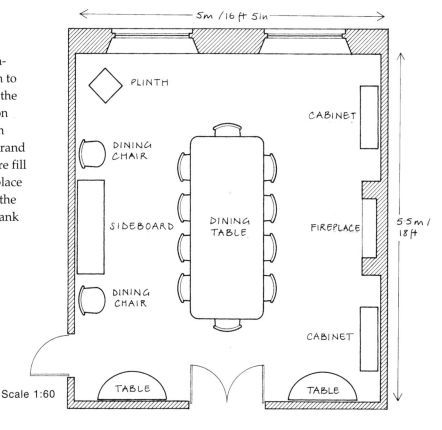

DESIGN DECISIONS

1 **Scheme** Green has been chosen as the basis for this scheme in a south-facing room. The cooling effect of this colour is diluted by a traditionally styled, cream wallpaper bearing a trellis pattern covering the wall above dado level. Below the dado rail, green paint has been applied and the horizontals that this treatment creates help to lower a very high ceiling.

2 **Flooring** Beige Wilton carpet fitted to close cover has a luxurious feel and provides a soft background against which the stunning table setting is seen.

3 **Window treatment** Generously proportioned windows provide a perfect setting for a grand swags-and-tails treatment. A tartan silk has been used to line the tails and trim the leading edge of the curtains and a deep bullion fringe finishes the swags. The loss of natural light from this curtain style is acceptable in a room facing south and having such handsomely proportioned windows. The brightness is further filtered by the use of sheers.

4 **Lighting** The dramatic effect of focused lighting from downlighters above the table is softened at night when candles within hurricane lamps are lit.

5 **Dining chairs** A stunning green-and-beige fabric has been used for the upholstery and it is shown off well on these high-backed chairs. The antique close-nailed finish to the backs and seats reinforces the room's traditional style.

6 **Tableware** Continuing the period theme, cut glass and fine china have been laid out with napkins to complement the scheme.

7 **Flowers** An important ingredient to dress any dining room and to perfume the air, the flowers on the table and mantel reflect the room colour scheme, while topiary trees of dried flowers complete the window dressing.

Family Dining

Family dining is all about happy, relaxed times spent enjoying wholesome food with family members. It is not about going into a cold, little-used, unwelcoming room where ritualistic behaviour is required. Family meals may provide the only time in the day when all gather together and proper conversation is possible, so it is vital to make this assembly as convenient, enjoyable and relaxing as possible. Decorations chosen with this in mind will go a long way to encourage just such an atmosphere.

For the space to work it needs to be practical, so that a glass of spilt juice does not cause a catastrophe or dropped food a drama. In this regard your choice of floor covering may be critical. A hard floor, from a maintenance viewpoint, is ideal. Ceramic or terracotta tiles may be easy to clean, but perhaps a little hard on the feet and noisy. A cushioned flooring of sheet vinyl, cork tiles or wood may be a more comfortable solution and one that is slightly warmer in appearance. If you have a partiality for soft finishes, an area rug that can be easily cleaned may be the answer. A fitted carpet is not out of bounds – especially if treated (when new) with a sealant to prevent the absorption of spills. Natural floorings are not recommended for families with anything less than the best behaved children – they tend to absorb liquids (unless treated) and hold crumbs and their unstable character can cause them to ruck up where chairs are dragged over their surface.

Other surfaces within the dining area may need to be child-proof too. A table with a laminate surface that can be cleaned very easily is one answer, and a wooden one, treated with a clear varnish, will perform almost as well. Should your table surface be of not such a suitable material, the use of an oil cloth will help to protect it. Always provide mats (cork or padded fabric are a good choice) for hot plates.

Neutral furnishings in this practical family dining area allow the many beautiful wood finishes to shine through.

Where smaller children are involved, it pays to use a resilient wall finish should this be within 'firing distance'. Gloss or other washable paint is suitable, as is vinyl wallpaper or wooden boarding.

When considering the decorations for a family dining area, you will, of course, also need to take into account any other purposes for which the room is intended. Wherever a family dining area is located, (near a food preparation area, for preference) the aim should be to create a space that is bright, cheerful and informal.

The lighting in a family dining room needs to be relatively bright and perhaps less dramatic than in a formal dining room. The dining table may well also be used for other purposes – homework, hobbies and so on, and these activities require good lighting con-ditions. A pendant fitting (or two, in the case of a long table) would be suitable, provided that either the bulb is not visible or that it is of the crown-silvered variety. It may be wise to avoid table-top lighting as it may interfere with work and hobbies, although this could be brought out for evening entertainment purposes.

To define your dining area it may be necessary to divide this portion of the room from the rest. You can do this in a variety of ways. A piece of furniture (such as a sideboard, a floor-to-ceiling shelf unit or a kitchen unit) could be placed appropriately between the two functions; an area rug, somewhat larger in size than the table, could be laid under the eating position; or screens could be used to obscure the cooking area of a kitchen.

How the room might look

THE PLAN

This medium-sized room is visually enlarged by the glazed doors opening it up to the adjacent space. Perfectly suited to the needs of a growing family, the table is well proportioned to the size of room and ample storage space is provided in the dresser and sideboard opposite. The symmetry has been maintained by the central positioning of the table, giving this room a casual but controlled feel.

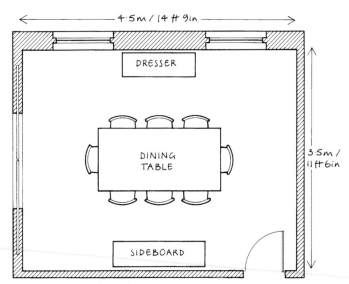

Scale 1:60

DESIGN DECISIONS

1 **Scheme** The neutral scheme based on natural materials in the dining room is repeated in the adjoining sitting room, which helps to make the two areas work well together.

2 **Flooring** Not only is parquet wood a highly practical finish but it also echoes the light colour of the wood of the table, chairs, dresser and sideboard, helping to harmonize the scheme.

3 **Table** Well weighted and sturdy, this timber table happily accommodates eight in comfort and visually loses its bulk against a background of a similar colour.

4 Chairs A harlequin set of similarly styled chairs is more interesting than a matching set and is much more fun to assemble. Tie-on cushions aid comfort and can be easily removed for cleaning when required.

5 Dresser Traditional in style, this gives the room a country look and provides useful storage for tableware.

6 Sideboard Placed opposite the dresser, this provides additional storage and maintains a sense of symmetry.

7 Windows A stained-glass panel rests within the frame of each of the two windows to provide a decorative statement.

8 Window treatment Curtains are slotted on a brass pole running the whole length of one wall. Unlined, they allow sunlight to filter through, giving the room a light and airy feel.

9 Double doors These glazed, sliding doors provide a division when required and slot neatly within the adjoining walls when drawn back. The glazing allows light to pass between the two rooms when the doors are closed.

10 Lighting Rise-and-fall pendant lights, providing convenient illumination for dining or doing homework, can be adjusted upwards when more overall lighting is required.

11 Plants These reinforce the country message.

Occasional Dining

As dining rooms are increasingly requisitioned for what are seen as priority uses – as a study, a playroom, a guest bedroom or a nursery – we are having to become ever more ingenious in seeking out a space for dining activities. Even if a dedicated space already exists, there may still be a call for some small corner for dinner *à deux* or even for solo suppers.

What, then, are the possibilities? In a living room a coffee table might be utilized for a casual television supper with friends, or perhaps a small round table normally covered with a full-length cloth could be given a new role as the centrepiece of a smart dinner for four. That often-neglected area, the hallway, offers many possibilities. Two semi-circular tables normally positioned separately against a wall and displaying collections of pretty things might be joined together to form a round table for a smart supper for six. A kitchen peninsular unit plus several stools might provide an easy space for an informal lunch with friends, and a garden suite in a conservatory could become the site of magical midsummer candlelit suppers.

Where space is limited, there are several measures that can be taken to make the area seem larger:

▶ A small dark basement room with a door leading to a garden can be transformed with the help of sheet mirror attached to the walls and faced with garden trellis. A suite of well-upholstered garden furniture, lots of shade-loving foliage and dozens of candles complete the picture.

▶ Banquette seating takes up far less space than individual chairs – an excellent way of creating a dining area within a bay window or small kitchen corner. In addition, if the seats are constructed with hinged tops, the space beneath can be used for long-term storage.

▶ A glass-top table will virtually disappear against background decorations and will not dominate the space it occupies.

▶ A good idea from the Shaker movement is to incorporate a peg rail into a room scheme. These are excellent for storing fold-up tables, chairs and other items when not in use.

▶ For occasional larger parties, a small round table can be temporarily extended with the help of a hinged circular top made of MDF (medium-density fibreboard) or similar weighty material in a size in excess of the existing top.

▶ Other space-saving tables are: drop-sided tables; tables that will accommodate additional drop-in leaves; gate-legged tables; trestle tables.

Accommodating dining chairs when they are not in use can be a problem in a small apartment. A great idea is to scatter them throughout your rooms, covering each drop-in seat with a fabric to match the scheme of the room where the chair is located. When they are gathered together for dining purposes, the chairs can be transformed with temporary covers all made of the same fabric to give the appearance of a matching set.

The quickest and easiest way to inject a transient eating area with a sense of occasion is by clever use of focused lighting. A floor-standing swing-arm lamp directed over the table will do the trick, as will a group of candles massed at the centre of the table and scattered around the room. A floor-standing uplighter placed in a corner behind a large plant will create some evening magic. Remember that by focusing light on the table, the room's main purpose will be to some extent disguised.

Neo-classicism is the theme for this grand hallway in a Mediterranean villa that happily changes its role to that of dining area for up to twenty people grouped around the two tables.

How the room might look

THE PLAN

The hallway is entered from a portico on the left and acts as a lobby to the grand salon to the right. A small sitting room is located at the top of the plan and opposite is an entrance to the kitchen – a perfect arrangement both for every day and when entertaining. In the classical style, symmetry permeates the plan, giving the room a great sense of order. When it is used in its capacity of dining room for a large party, the two granite-top tables are set with fine china and lit by candles. The side tables are used for serving and additional chairs are gathered from other locations in the villa.

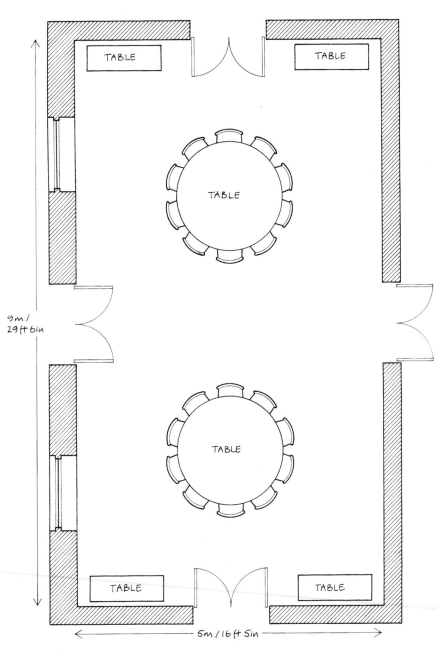

Scale 1:60

DESIGN DECISIONS

1 **Scheme** Deliberately neutral to contrast with the boldly coloured schemes of the rooms which lead off from it, this large space is made more intimate by the colour rendering of both walls and ceiling in the same pale corn hue.

2 **Flooring** Teak, bush-hammered stone and brown glazed tiles combine geometrically to form this dramatic entrance-hall flooring which is both practical and attention-seeking. The pattern is enclosed in a border of the plain stone to ease the transition to other floor surfaces in the rooms leading off.

3 **Architectural details** An over-scaled broken cornice, keystones and bold architraves add impact to the room and reinforce the classical theme.

4 **Doors** Four sets of almost full-height double doors give the room a sense of importance and grandly frame the views beyond.

5 Tables Two granite-top round tables with plaster tripod bases provide a surface for books and baskets of dried flowers in their everyday role and can each seat ten people for large dinner parties.

6 Chairs English-style Portuguese chairs with a limed finish are scattered throughout the house and assembled whenever a large dinner party is planned.

7 Side tables Two classically inspired tables with stone tops sit at either end of the room to provide a surface for decorative objects during the day and serving areas for dinners at night.

8 Mirrors Flanking the double doors into the salon, these two highly decorative, gilt looking-glasses from the eighteenth century bring a sparkle and sense of occasion to the room, especially when candles are lit at night. They are carefully positioned to reflect the attractive exterior view and help to amplify the natural light in this otherwise slightly dim area.

9 Pictures Twenty splatter-work silhouettes from the mid-eighteenth century litter the walls in a symmetrical fashion, all positioned with a common baseline.

BEDROOMS

It is quite extraordinary to think that we devote so little attention to the planning of a room where we are likely to spend half our day if not half our life! Of all the rooms in a house the bedroom is perhaps the most important – a private space in which we can recoup and recharge our batteries, ready to face the onslaught of another day.

We think nothing of spending endless hours on the careful planning of a kitchen. It may not occur to us that the bedroom requires every bit as much attention. But the positioning of a dressing table and the establishment of the correct depth for a wardrobe are equally as critical for our comfort and convenience as deciding on the height of worktops and a location for the refrigerator.

Listing the activities that will be taking place in the bedroom is the starting point. Apart from the obvious one of sleeping, we may, for instance, wish to be able to read, exercise, take breakfast, write letters, or play or work on a computer. Chronicling these at the start of your design project will help concentrate the mind – because it is not until these have been established that you can plan for the space, lighting, furnishing and storage facilities each requires.

FURNISHINGS

The bed is the main item of furniture in the room and should always be considered first. It is best sited where there is sufficient room to manoeuvre around it (a minimum of 45cm/1ft 6in is recommended), where there is good natural light and from where there is a pleasant view. Other considerations are the electrical points (can the existing ones be utilized in

'Less is more' – demonstrated by designer David Hicks in this Portuguese villa guest bedroom dressed in shades of white on white.

the new arrangement?) and, not to be forgotten, in which position will the bed look best when viewed upon entering the room?

Careful thought should also go into the choice of bed head. Wood and metal are currently favoured materials, but are comfortable only if plenty of pillows are also supplied. A padded type, provided it is covered with a resilient or patterned fabric, may be a more suitable selection. A decorator's tip is to attach the bed head to the wall instead of to the bed itself: this will result in a more stable bed head and will mean easier bed-making.

The most important considerations when it comes to the choice of bed cover are how it will look when in place, and how it will fare when folded. Quilting a fine fabric will do much to give it body and will help preserve its new appearance for longer, and having a suitable receptacle at the end of the bed on to which to fold back the spread will also encourage good care. A long stool will serve the purpose, but a blanket box will have the added advantage of providing storage for cushions and extra blankets.

STORAGE

In a bedroom there is so much to accommodate and never enough space. A walk-in closet is undoubtedly the most practical solution, but not always an option for those owning a smaller or older property. Additional storage capacity may have to be found wherever possible. Perhaps a cupboard could be located in the hallway outside the room or an adjacent small bedroom converted into a dressing room?

Clothes are likely to be the most pressing problem, with the need to store items both horizontally on shelves and vertically on hangers. Hangers require a space approximately 60cm/2ft deep, and it is important to position the rail at a height which will allow for garments to clear the base of the cupboard. A

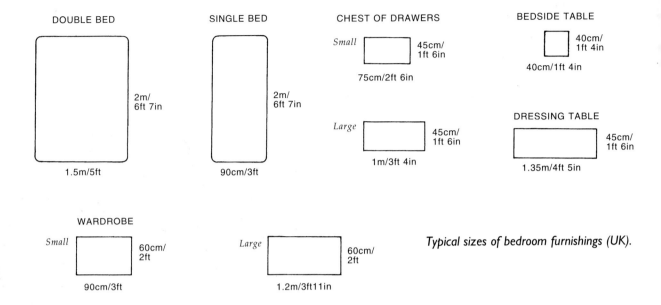

DOUBLE BED
2m/6ft 7in
1.5m/5ft

SINGLE BED
2m/6ft 7in
90cm/3ft

CHEST OF DRAWERS
Small
45cm/1ft 6in
75cm/2ft 6in

Large
45cm/1ft 6in
1m/3ft 4in

BEDSIDE TABLE
40cm/1ft 4in
40cm/1ft 4in

DRESSING TABLE
45cm/1ft 6in
1.35m/4ft 5in

WARDROBE
Small
60cm/2ft
90cm/3ft

Large
60cm/2ft
1.2m/3ft 11in

Typical sizes of bedroom furnishings (UK).

system of wire baskets within a framework could offer the most flexible shelf solution (and, being free-standing, could travel with you when you move on).

A built-in wardrobe unit spanning floor to ceiling will generally provide greater capacity than a free-standing cupboard. This built-in type of housing can also be more easily disguised if you apply the same treatment to the door fronts as to the walls of the room (even going so far as to run the cornice and skirting details along the top and bottom).

LIGHTING

In many ways the rules applying to lighting the living room can be applied to the bedroom too, but perhaps in a more subtle fashion. It is important to create a calm restful atmosphere and to avoid glare. Light diffused by the addition of silk shades will give just the right soft glow.

As well as achieving a relaxing mood, it is also vital to ensure that the 'task' lighting is doing its job. Of primary concern must be the bedside lighting. Position here is everything: the light source should be at least 60cm/2ft above mattress height if the 'hotel bedroom syndrome' is to be avoided (where the carpet by the bed is beautifully illuminated, but there is simply no chance of any of those rays reaching our book in bed!). Buying a sufficiently tall bedside table

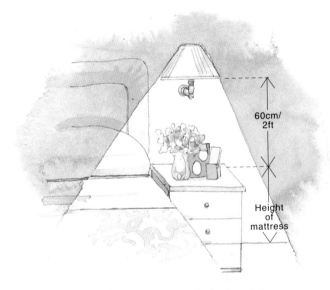

60cm/2ft

Height of mattress

Example of correct position for bedside light.

(of, say, approximately 50cm/1ft 8in for the average mattress height) is a good starting point and, so long as the light source is at a sufficient height, it does not matter whether this is a free-standing table lamp, a wall fitting or a headboard-mounted lamp. Many consider the angle-arm wall fitting to be the perfect answer. This frees the bedside table space and can be adjusted for reading in bed or swung back against the wall for bed-making. For double occupancy,

separate lights to each side of the bed will allow one person to sleep undisturbed while the other reads in bed. These lights, for the sake of convenience, should be two-way-switched between bedside and entrance door so that they can be illuminated on entering the room and extinguished from the bedside .

If a downlighter or pendant fitting is used to provide general lighting, ensure that this is not positioned too near the bed head or the glare will be visible by anyone in the resting position.

Locating a dressing table in front of a window certainly helps with day-time grooming, but at night it will be necessary to ensure that there is an adequate light source between the person sitting at the dressing

Stars painted on the ceiling of this gorgeous blue-and-cream bedroom are reflected in the lantern hanging from its centre.

table and the mirror. Twin candle lamps provide an excellent solution. The same applies for a full-length mirror, although in this case wall lights to either side or a downlighter fixed directly above may be the answer.

Strip lights fitted within wardrobes and with an automatic switch in the door jamb will make the selection of clothing much easier. Alternatively, and provided that the cupboard door exteriors are attractive, a ceiling-fixed wall washer will serve the same purpose.

Main Bedroom

As our lives become ever more frenetic, the haven a bedroom offers becomes more and more inviting – and not just for sleeping. Quiet reading, television viewing (for the programmes *we* want to watch!), enjoying a peaceful light supper, letter writing – these are all activities that may be best suited to that special private space. Whether accompanied by a partner or not, we should consider our own bedroom the one area where we are obliged to please no one but ourselves (the words indulgence and pampering spring to mind). It therefore makes good sense for the 'best' bedroom space available in terms of area, shape, view, orientation and access to dressing and bathroom facilities to be reserved for this purpose.

At last the benefits of self-containment have been realized. We expect to pay a premium for a hotel suite, so why not plan permanent accommodation on similar lines, with areas set aside for hobbies, relaxing, dressing, bathing and of course sleeping?

When it comes to deciding upon a scheme, it really is a question of whatever takes your fancy: remember, this is *your* room! For preference, though, many people opt for soft colours and quiet patterns as these are considered less tiring on the eyes and more conducive to rest and relaxation (see pages 12–13). An obvious area of contention is when two people of different persuasions try to concoct a scheme to suit both. This problem can usually be overcome by the skilful selection of colours and patterns mid-way between the two tastes. Botanical prints do not necessarily mean acres of pretty pink roses, and in any case pink does not have to be pale and feminine. Some of the most successful bedroom schemes rely on neither interesting colours nor bold patterns. Picked for their blandness, neutrals provide a wonderful backdrop for relaxation and can be sparked up by the introduction

Cream forms a calming background for this fresh country-house-comes-to-town scheme.

of pretty bed linen, stylish furniture and sharp accessories. Here you have the chance to buy that really fine, delicately coloured carpet of your dreams (thought to be far too impractical for other traffic-heavy areas). The one requirement is that, whatever covering is selected, it should be kind on the feet. Fashionably modern, natural floorings rarely meet this criterion, but the situation can be saved by laying mats of softer, more friendly materials at bedside 'landing spots'.

There are many styles of dressing table, among which the fabric-covered type is a timeless favourite. The most important factor, however, is its positioning so that as much natural light as possible falls upon the face of the person sitting at the dressing table – beneath a window is ideal.

If you enjoy the feeling of being cocooned, bed drapes are for you. Whether emanating from a corona, half-tester or full tester, they give a wonderfully secure, enclosed feeling and look extremely attractive into the bargain. Always devote careful thought to the lining of any such bed treatment as that is what will be most often seen by the person lying in bed. A smaller repeat of the face fabric pattern can produce a very pleasing result, as can the use of ticking fabric in a co-ordinating colour.

Everyone has their personal preference when it comes to the choice of bedside table or cupboard. There are, though, some common principles worth considering. First, for convenience, it is best if the unit is approximately the same height as the top of the bed mattress. This will vary, but will most usually be around 50cm/1ft 8in. Ideally there should be enough space within the unit to accommodate all that you might wish to store at the bedside: this will help prevent a cluttered top with nowhere to set down that occasional cup of tea or perhaps a posy of fresh rosebuds. A sheet of clear glass cut to the outline of the top of a cloth-covered table will help to prevent staining and dust gathering on the fabric surface.

How the room might look

THE PLAN

The bed is positioned facing an attractive conversation grouping of sofa and easy chair and provides a good view of the garden through the bay window. The availability of natural light was the determining factor when locating the dressing table. Two antique chairs to either side of this complete the group. The sofa is flanked on one side by a cloth-covered circular table (a suitable site for a lamp) and on the other by a bookcase to house reading matter. The coffee table provides a useful surface for magazines, flowers and meal trays. On the left-hand wall a built-in cupboard spanning nearly its full length provides approximately 4m/13ft of storage divided into shelving and hanging space with long-term storage above. A 'corridor' between the cupboard and the rest of the furnishings has been deliberately left to allow easy passage to the adjoining small dressing room and bathroom.

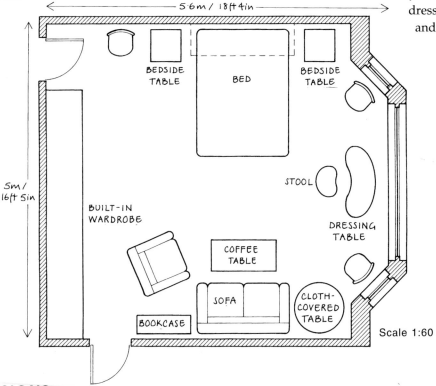

DESIGN DECISIONS

1 **Scheme** Everything an ideal bedroom scheme should seek to be – clean, calm, light, balanced and relaxing. The floral print helps to bring the garden element into the room.

2 **Main fabric** Controlled use of the floral pattern on the walls and for the bed treatment is balanced by masses of plain fabric to prevent the scheme from appearing too busy. Unusually, the patterned fabric is used to line the inside of the drapes, while plain fabric is used for the exterior.

3 **Fabric-covered walls** These help to cushion noise, giving the room a hushed luxurious feel. Fixings are concealed by a smart dark trim.

4 **Carpet** The choice of cream, a rash decision in any other room where traffic is heavier, is perfectly apt here. The pale colour also helps to give the room a very light, airy feel.

5 **Bed treatment** The generously proportioned, decorative half-tester echoes the serpentine outline of the curtains, adding to a feeling of harmony.

6 Bed cover Fitted and box-style, its straight lines are in contrast to the frillier elements in the room.

7 Bed base Finely pleated, it perfectly finishes this pretty bed treatment.

8 Bedside tables Traditional in style, these painted tables are of a good height and just big enough to stow bedside necessities.

9 Dressing table Perfectly positioned for maximum natural light. The kidney shape of the table is replicated in the accompanying stool.

10 Curtain and bed valance headings Deep smocking gives interest to these perfectly proportioned but otherwise plain curtains. A pretty navy-and-cream fan edging neatly finishes the base.

11 Chairs The positioning of these against a pale background helps to emphasize the magnificent curves of the chair backs.

12 Lighting The bedside lamps carry a light source at a suitable height for reading in bed and the use of silk coolie shades helps to spread and diffuse the light.

Occasional Guest Bedroom

A world-famous hotelier is reputed to commission the decoration of his hotel bedrooms only after the interior designer has produced a mock-up of the proposed scheme and after he, the hotel group president, has slept in the sample room for two nights. These are extreme measures for a host to take to ensure the comfort of his guests, but should we do anything less for the enjoyment of our personal visitors?

Few households these days can afford to dedicate bedroom space for the exclusive use of a sporadic guest. Space in many houses will simply not permit it and, more often than not, this room will have to double up with some other function. A study or dressing room could probably most easily be converted to serve this additional purpose with the minimum of disruption, or perhaps a little-used dining room might be considered. Whichever space is selected, take care not to compromise the room's main purpose to any degree for the sake of the occasional visitor. With clever planning it should be possible to devise a room to take on both roles without difficulty.

Should you ever wish to issue an impromptu invitation for an overnight stay, it is important that the room can be readied quickly – no guests like to think that they are putting a host/hostess to any trouble. The conversion therefore needs to be achieved without major furniture movements or storage adjustments.

Beds, when not in use, can be disguised in a variety of ways:

▶ Convertible chair- and sofa-beds are sold in their thousands and are extremely popular, but be aware that some seating comfort may be compromised by the bed mechanism.

▶ The fold-away type which emerges, ready-made, from a wall cupboard is easy to erect and is unobtrusive when not in use.

▶ A fold-up camp bed is cheap and useful for visiting children, but may not offer sufficient comfort for an adult. There is also the problem of housing the bed when it is not in use.

▶ A day bed is for many the most satisfactory solution. When dressed with bolsters during the day, it provides useful seating and can be handsomely draped for decorative impact. Bedding may be contained within drawers beneath the divan or in a separate blanket box or chest.

▶ If your need is to provide for two guests, one of the best solutions is a bed with collapsible legs which slips beneath a second bed when not required.

Lighting in this dual-purpose room needs to be carefully thought through if it is to serve both uses adequately. Incorporating free-standing lights such as table lamps and standard lamps (see page 10) will allow you to make swift minor adjustments to your arrangement. Always ensure that there is some form of lighting which can be switched from the bedside.

A wash basin in a guest room is a boon, giving independence to the guest and relieving pressure on a family bathroom. A nearby radiator could have a temporary rack attached for holding towels and a folding screen might be employed to hide the basin when it is not in use.

If the dual role of the room is to be disguised, good storage will be needed. A desk in a study might house stationery, and when the room is required as a bedroom, this could be covered with a full-length cloth and a mirror placed on top for use as a dressing table. Where there is no room for a wardrobe, a coat stand or hooks on the back of a door should suffice for the short stayer. Somewhere will be needed to set down a suitcase. A folding luggage rack, painted to co-ordinate with your scheme and crossed with pretty braid, is an ideal solution.

A vision in red, this study-cum-guest room offers a warm welcome, even on the coldest of nights.

Having a guest in your home is all about giving pleasure – those little touches that count for so much:

▶ Guest towels sprayed with cologne and presented in a basket on the end of the bed.

▶ Fresh flowers on a dressing table.

▶ A decanter of mineral water and small tin of biscuits freshly provided by the bedside.

▶ Recent magazines or children's story books left on a small table.

▶ Tea/coffee-making facilities (the kettle must be small enough to be filled from a basin tap) on a tray placed near a socket.

▶ A television, radio and alarm clock for entertainment and information.

▶ A hair dryer in a dressing-table drawer.

▶ A mirror – full-length, if possible, to aid grooming.

▶ A basket of bathroom goodies – perfumes, shampoo and so on, plus a minute bottle of detergent for washing 'smalls' (airline and hotel give-aways are perfect for this purpose).

How the room might look

THE PLAN

This useful space was eked out of a central London maisonette to provide both a work area and accommodation for an occasional overnight guest. The sofa doubles as a bed, and opposite a wall of deep shelves and cupboards houses files and books. The room is also used as a small sitting room, and entertainment is provided by a television and audio system concealed within the wall units.

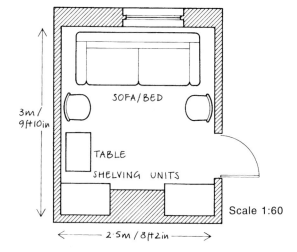

DESIGN DECISIONS

1 **Scheme** Warmth is introduced to counteract the cool light entering a north-facing room by the use of bold brilliant red in this monochromatic scheme.

2 **Sofa** Covered in a red-and-white pattern to relieve the masses of solid red, this quickly converts to a bed when required. As a sofa, it is perfectly positioned for television viewing.

3 **Chairs** Positioned at either end of the sofa, a pair of folding wood and cane chairs double up as bedside tables.

4 **Window treatment** A festoon curtain with a handsome swag softens the light entering through the large window. An Indian-inspired pattern is used and is reflected in the ornaments below. A border in a darker red provides definition.

5 **Lighting** Lots of lighting is needed in this room, where the wall surfaces are finished in a dark matt colour. A pair of wall lights, created by the designer, reflect the architectural subject of the prints and are the right height for reading in bed.

6 **Prints** Old architectural prints are mounted on red card to link them to the scheme.

AN ALTERNATIVE GUEST ROOM

DESIGN DECISIONS

Scheme Neutral and elegant, the scheme encourages the eye to rest upon the attractive view of the garden beyond.

Flooring Off-white ceramic tiles 30cm/12in square have been laid diagonally for added interest and are a perfect surface to lead out into the garden.

Cupboard Handsomely styled, this cupboard gives few hints of its contents.

This simply decorated hallway gives no hint of its dual role — until the cupboard doors are opened.

Lighting Uplighters positioned in the corners throw into relief the contours of two pretty chairs. General lighting is provided by the pendant light. When the space is used as a bedroom, integral downlighters illuminate the bed-head area for night-time reading.

Elderly Person's Bed-sit

Having an elderly relative living in your home can often benefit the whole family. The cost of professional care is becoming beyond the reach of many and, for the older person, living with an extended family can provide continued interest, security and the best possible care. The accommodation of a member of a different generation within the home, it has to be admitted, is potentially fraught, but with a little care and good planning this should not prove to be too disruptive.

The room you choose for the older person will, ideally, be at ground level so as to minimize difficult journeys and should if possible allow space for more than just sleeping. If it also has a large window with an interesting view, this should make your decision easy. The provision of areas for relaxing, bathing, cooking and dining will allow the senior citizen to remain active and somewhat independent from the rest of the household – a situation that is likely to suit both parties. Dividing these areas of activity (by employing screens, curtains or items of furniture) is important for the occupant so that he/she can appreciate the changes in his/her day and can entertain without private areas being on view.

Designing a room for an elderly person is best done by placing yourself in that person's shoes and by thinking through how to compensate for the possible limitations imposed upon their lifestyle. You don't want to be too pessimistic, but it also pays to plan for days when the person's capacities may be reduced. Some of the more obvious provisions are:

▶ A comfortable, easy-to-get-out-of chair for the room occupant and seating for guests.

▶ Bright lighting to help cope with failing sight. Wall and ceiling-fixed lights plus well-weighted table and floor-standing lamps are suitable. A bedside switch is helpful, as is a low-wattage light that can be left on overnight. Remember to highlight any changes in floor level. Perhaps also consider positioning sockets and switches nearer to hand height.

▶ Warmth – older people generally require warmer temperatures than the young. Central-heating radiators and open fires need to be easily controlled and well guarded.

▶ Storage at an easily accessed level and with openings that are not too difficult to operate.

▶ The elimination of all sharp corners for safety reasons, and the removal of any electrical cables that could be tripped over. A smoke alarm is another wise precaution.

▶ In the bathroom, grab rails and a lockable medicine cupboard. You might also like to consider fitting an 'engaged' door sign rather than a lock. Mixer taps and a controlled-temperature shower system will help avoid extremes of water temperature.

▶ Curtains on a corded track, operated from the side, to ease opening and closing.

▶ Non-slip flooring and well-attached loose coverings. A fitted carpet of the type that can be easily cleaned is ideal.

The decoration of the room in a familiar style (most likely to be traditional) and the incorporation of existing possessions will help to make the elderly person feel quickly at home. Inviting them to make decoration choices will involve them further. Pretty patterns and cheerful colours will do much to lift their mood and the addition of plants and even a pet will bring life to the room. In addition certain electrical gadgets, such as remote control for lights and curtains, could well smooth the life of an elderly person.

Country casual is the theme for this comfortable all-purpose room for an elderly person.

How the room might look

THE PLAN

The view upon entering this well-planned self-contained accommodation for an elderly person is of the comfortable sitting area straight ahead. To the left units enclose the kitchen area. The bedroom area is cleverly divided from the sitting room by means of a high-backed banquette seating unit and next to the bathroom is a useful dressing area containing a wardrobe and full-length mirror.

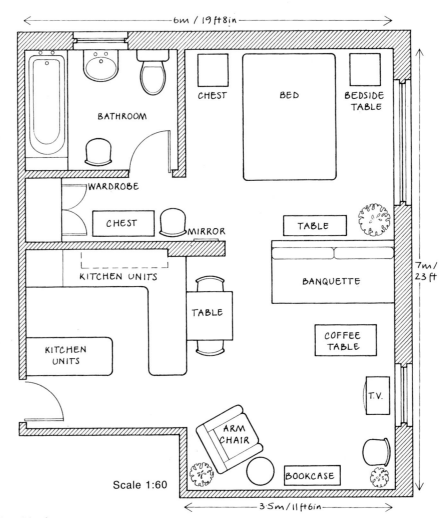

Scale 1:60

DESIGN DECISIONS

1 **Scheme** Cream walls provide a blank canvas against which country-inspired decorations are displayed. Warm colours predominate and are encapsulated in the border that runs around the sitting room at picture-rail height and which is echoed in the bedroom at dado height.

2 **Flooring** Non-slip ceramic floor tiles in a warm terracotta tone run throughout the space. In the sitting room an oriental rug defines a conversation grouping and is echoed by a smaller one next to the bed.

3 **Banquette seating** Ideal for visiting guests, this seating arrangement is so positioned to partition off the bedroom area. Easily converted into a bed, it is useful for overnight guests or perhaps, in years to come, could provide accommodation for a carer. The base stores bed linens and pillows.

4 **Table** Perfectly sized for the lone diner or small group, this sturdy pine table fits in conveniently next to the kitchen.

5 **Chairs** Continuing the country theme, these have rush seats and a soft cushion for that bit of extra comfort.

6 **Kitchen shelves** The height of these shelves and their lack of door fronts mean that items can easily be reached by an elderly person.

7 **Windows** Stretching almost from ceiling to floor, these large windows provide a generous view of the garden (especially from the bed) and ensure that the room is rarely gloomy. On sunny days the windows can be slid back and entrance to the garden gained.

8 **Window treatment** A blind, headed by a length of paper border on the wall above, gives the windows a simple out-of-the-way treatment.

9 **Lighting** Traditional in feel, the various fittings give a warm glow to the room while ensuring that tasks are targeted. In the bedroom area a bedside lamp is easily reached at night and a Victorian pendant light improves the overall light level. The sitting room is lit by a similar combination and in the kitchen area a candle lamp casts light on the nearby dining table.

10 **Wall clock** Without a busy programme, an elderly person can easily lose track of time: this pretty ceramic clock will act as a helpful reminder.

11 **Flowers** Both dried and fresh, these reinforce the country theme and bring life to the room.

BATHROOMS

The greatest test of a good bathroom is to ask yourself whether you like to linger there. If the answer is no, it's time to convert that cold, sad, clinical space into something much more pleasurable.

Why the bathroom should be given such low priority by most people and why architects and developers pay so little attention to this vital room is a mystery. Often allocated the meanest of budgets and constructed from what little space remains after all the 'important' rooms have been decided upon, the typical bathroom is frequently small, misshapen and possessing the very worst of views (if, indeed, it has a window at all). From this it can be deduced that we need to be very skilful if we are to create a warm practical room that invites us in.

If you are in a position to start from scratch, you have a wonderful opportunity to customize the space to your exact requirements. Allocate to a bathroom the largest area you can afford and position it for your convenience, even if this means sacrificing a rarely used guest room. Then decide exactly what functions you want the room to perform. These days, as well as being a room for bathing, it may well be used for exercising, beauty treatments, child's play, dressing, reading and relaxing as well as functioning, in some cases, as a laundry.

The placement of the essential equipment of a bathroom is critical – decorations can be changed at whim, but the bath, WC and wash basin will outlive many a scheme. To help you decide upon the best positions, draw up a scaled plan on graph paper (see pages 5–7) and be sure to have this checked out by a specialist plumber before proceeding further. It may well be that by lining up all your equipment on one wall, less disruption will be caused and a smaller proportion of your budget spent. Consider rehanging the entrance door on the opposite axis if this will aid your plan. Alternatively a sliding door or double doors may give you those vital extra few centimetres which will allow you to accommodate all that you need. The space around each item of equipment requires careful planning too, if you wish to carry out the various functions in comfort. Don't forget to consider also how things will work when more than one person is occupying the space (see page 84).

Convention dictates that the bath should run along a wall, but why not be adventurous and place it coming out into the room from a wall or even position it in the centre of the room? Not a new idea this – some of the first baths were so placed to be near an open fire. On which subject, if you have the opportunity to retain an existing fireplace or to construct a new one, think how cosy this could make your bathroom.

The bathroom is a perfect place for incorporating fitted furniture. Not only will it help to hide away much of the 'engineering', but it will also give your room a smarter, more tailored appearance. Incidentally, never overlook the view that you will get while sitting in the bath – from that low level much that is not particularly attractive (the underside of the basins and so on) is revealed.

Some bathrooms need little more than a face lift. In such cases the addition of co-ordinating towels, the introduction of a carpet or the adjustment of lighting systems can sometimes transform at little cost. Ugly dominant ceramic tiles can be disguised by painting over (see page 14) and a discoloured bath re-enamelled. Sometimes a bathroom can take on a new lease of life if you simply clear away the clutter. Enclose the basin in a vanity unit or attach a wall cabinet and much of the bathroom paraphernalia

Pleated silk shades surround brass wall lamps and are echoed in the mirror-framed Roman shade at the window. Brown walls show off the beautifully figured marble vanity top.

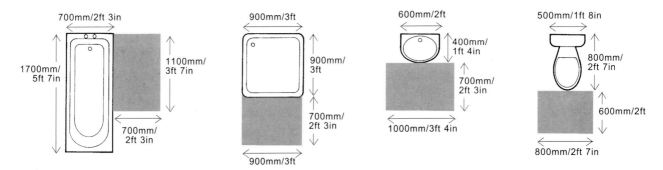

Typical sizes of bathroom fitments and recommended spaces for activity.

can be stored out of view, greatly improving the overall effect.

The choice of style for your bathroom is very much a personal decision. As with all other rooms, if you follow the architectural style/period of your house or apartment, you probably won't go far wrong. Many fittings from bygone eras are still being reproduced: an Art Deco-inspired bathroom, for instance, in a 1920s or 1930s house could look stunning. One thing to avoid is a colourful over-stylized bathroom suite that will not only date but will also limit future schemes.

When it comes to thinking about the decorative details, a tired palm, fluffy loo seat cover, 'fishy' plastic shower curtains and a dish of broken shells will not suffice! Not only are these features hackneyed, but they bear little relation to each other and add up to nothing short of a mess. Instead choose a theme for your room and follow it through.

SURFACES

Wall coverings must, above all, perform well in humid conditions. Papers can be used but must be securely fixed and have a spongable surface if they are to survive. Non-vinyl papers can be rendered more resilient if coated with a layer of clear varnish. Around basins, showers and baths a sheet of clear acrylic can be fixed to form a transparent splashback. If marble is used, care should be taken to ensure that protruding corners have polished edges. More popular choices are ceramic tiles (aesthetically more pleasing when full-height) or paint. Ceramic tiles can be used on the floor, but make sure that they are

specified for floor use and are of a non-slip variety. Alternative hard floor treatments are cork, marble, wood or cushioned vinyl. In each case the fewer the joins (where water can accumulate), the better. If covering a hard floor with a rug, ensure that it will not slip or trip anybody up. Carpet is also a popular choice: this is obviously softer on the feet but is less easily cleaned.

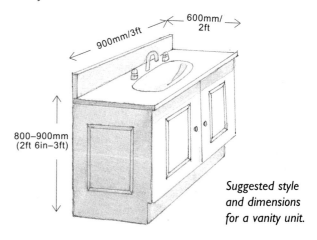

Suggested style and dimensions for a vanity unit.

FURNITURE

The basic items of the bathroom suite (bath and/or shower, WC, wash basin and optional bidet) will no doubt take up most of your budget and so should be carefully selected. A classic white or cream suite is often the preferred choice. Taps should be easy to manipulate, even with wet hands, and a mixer arrangement will aid temperature control. Roll-top Victorian-style baths with claw feet are a current favourite but should be reserved for the larger bathroom where they can be viewed to advantage. The panelled-in type is more common and gives a neat fitted look (especially if you can continue the skirting/wainscoting detail around the base of the unit). A vanity unit to surround the wash basin will give a similar effect, but in this case a recessed plinth is required (as for kitchen units) to enable the person using the basin to stand close to it. Be as generous as you can with the size of vanity unit to give plenty of elbow room when washing and to increase storage capacity. Apart from these essentials, other items to add to bathroom pleasure are: a heated towel rail; a chair or stool; and a chaise longue for ultimate luxury.

STORAGE

Most bathrooms suffer from a lack of storage, so it is no wonder that they appear cluttered and disorganized. In general, bathroom necessities are not attractive and display surfaces should be left free for more decorative items such as perfume bottles and so on. Bath cleaners and the like can be found a home in the base of a vanity unit if this is included in your scheme – behind doors or a curtain, these items remain handy but out of sight. Additional storage can be located in other fitments or a free-standing chest. A stool with towelling cover and lift-up seat combines a useful piece of furniture with extra storage space. Extra loo rolls don't have to be hidden away: heaped in a basket or other suitable container, they can take on decorative importance. How many times have you turned round in a hotel bathroom only to find no place to hang a dressing gown? Hooks on a door or wall space cost little and add considerably to convenience.

LIGHTING

As well as providing good 'working' light conditions, consider introducing hints of glamour – even perhaps Hollywood-style with 'film star' lighting around a mirror. Safety, however, must be your primary concern: whatever your choice of fitting, ensure that it has been passed for bathroom use. Safety also plays a role when it comes to switching and regulations may require that, if a switch is

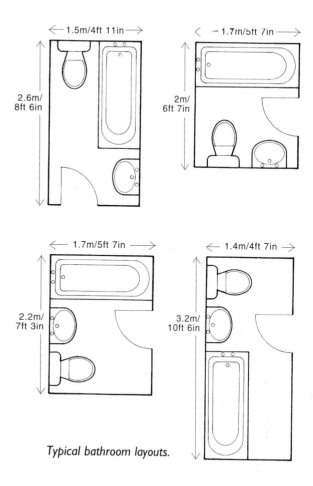

Typical bathroom layouts.

located within the bathroom, a pull-cord type is used. Low-voltage lights (with their transformers that help to isolate the fitting) are particularly suitable for bathroom use, and sockets, with the exception of specially designed shaver sockets, are not permitted at all within the bathroom.

Think carefully about the surfaces in your bathroom. They may well be white and have a polished reflective finish that will cause glare if overlit.

As suitable surfaces on which to attach lighting may well be limited, sealed bathroom-rated downlighters may prove to be the most useful fittings to light bathroom activities. As in the bedroom, ensure that light is positioned between the person using the mirror and the mirror itself. The standard fitting for this situation is a strip light, but a ceiling-fixed downlighter or wall lights to either side of the mirror may provide a more aesthetic solution.

En-suite Bathroom

Just as there is a trend towards connecting the kitchen with living/dining areas for social reasons, so it is with the bedroom and bathroom. As families become more and more fragmented because of increasing time spent away from home pursuing work, study and pastime commitments, time actually spent in the home has become a precious commodity and the desire for the company of family members strong. The en-suite bathroom in modern times is a necessity rather than a luxury. Not only does it allow for bathroom functions to be carried out in privacy, but provides a more companionable ambience if you wish.

If you are considering forming an en-suite bathroom where none has previously existed, you might think of cutting into the bedroom space if the conversion of an adjacent room is not feasible. If you choose to follow this route, take care not to compromise both rooms by spoiling the architecture of the bedroom and providing too small a space adequately to accommodate all the bathroom equipment you need. If space is very limited, building in a whole wall of cupboard units within the bedroom, one to house a basin and WC, another for a shower and perhaps a further one for hanging clothes may prove the most aesthetically pleasing configuration.

Because the en-suite bathroom is likely to be for the sole use of the occupant(s) of the adjacent bedroom, it can be tailored to their needs without consideration for others. The adult en-suite bathroom can be styled without regard to the assaults a family bathroom is likely to undergo. Wallpaper might be considered and the bedroom carpet continued into the bathroom (with mats to protect potentially wet areas). Pictures might be hung and more items of furniture incorporated. Drapes around the bath might also be considered. If this is your approach, ensure that there is adequate ventilation (to the exterior where practical) to prevent condensation. Internal bathrooms (without a window) are required to be vented and this is frequently operated automatically with the light switch.

If the bathroom and bedroom are to work successfully together, their schemes need to relate, while at the same time maintaining their own individual character. An effective way of achieving this is by reversing the bedroom scheme in the bathroom – that is, taking the bedroom accent colour and using this as the main colour for the bathroom, and adopting the main bedroom colour as an accent colour in the bathroom.

As more and more husbands and wives now both work, bathroom 'collisions' become increasingly likely. To prevent these it is a good idea,

Style, understatement and elegance – this classically inspired, user-friendly bathroom made for two has it all.

where space and budget permit, for facilities to be doubled up. A double sink arrangement, a bath and a shower and two WCs will all help to make preparations for the day or for sleep a speedier and more convenient process. For the ultimate in luxury, the inclusion of a dressing room in your suite, if at all possible, will not only free cupboard space in the bedroom but will also allow for one partner to dress without waking the other.

When planning a kitchen we are accustomed to thinking in terms of fitted furniture, so why not in the bathroom which also has to house unsightly equipment and cumbersome plumbing? A framed and panelled bath with drapes, a basin enclosed in a vanity unit, and built-in shelves around a hot water tank or to fill an awkward recess all help to relieve storage problems and give the bathroom a more streamlined profile.

How the room might look

THE PLAN

Perfectly arranged furnishings in this spacious bathroom provide amply for a busy couple with clashing schedules. Double doors at the entrance are faced with 'his' and 'hers' full-height mirrors and a decorative sofa forms a pleasing focal point upon entering the room. Twin basins beneath the window are well positioned to take maximum advantage of any natural light. Curtains at the entrances to the two WCs offer privacy and the centrally placed bath is easily accessed from either side. A shower in one of the WC cubicles offers an alternative bathing facility.

DESIGN DECISIONS

1 **Scheme** This cool, neutral, grey scheme is both calming and suggestive of classical times. Black accents have been introduced in the bath surround, WC seats, curtain poles, vanity top and picture frames to give the scheme definition.

2 **Theme** In this case, classical – as emphasized by the urn on the bath, the Piranese print, the dish on the vanity top and the vase of fresh lilies.

3 **Flooring** The choice of this off-white carpet is justified in this adult bathroom where wear and tear are likely to be minimal.

4 **Bath** Centrally placed, this adds to the classical symmetry of this smart bathroom.

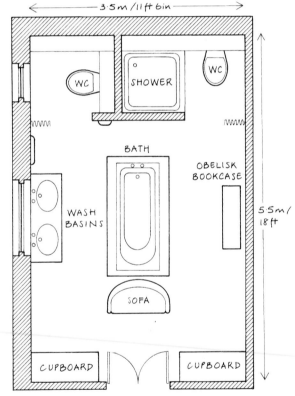

Scale 1:60

5 **Cupboards** Fitted storage cupboards to either side of the double entrance doors and beneath the basins ensure that clutter is housed out of view. An obelisk bookcase opposite the window accommodates bathtime reading matter.

6 WC cisterns These unsightly pieces of equipment in the two cubicles are neatly boxed in and hidden from view.

7 Lighting Principally provided by recessed down-lighters, this gives an otherwise fairly bland room added drama without making a feature of the fittings themselves. The value of the light from the downlighter over the bath (which is positioned slightly off-centre to avoid a structural beam in the ceiling) is intensified by reflection from the white enamel of the bath.

8 Skirting Notice how this continues around the fitted elements to give them the appearance of being integral.

9 Curtains At the entrance to the WCs and shower, these simply styled, goblet-headed curtains are suspended from decorative, crook-ended metal poles.

10 Towel rail Positioned vertically near the basins and easily accessed from the bath, this towel rail with heated bars ensures that towels are always warm and dry.

11 Telephone Essential for busy people, this colour-blending telephone is sited for maximum convenience.

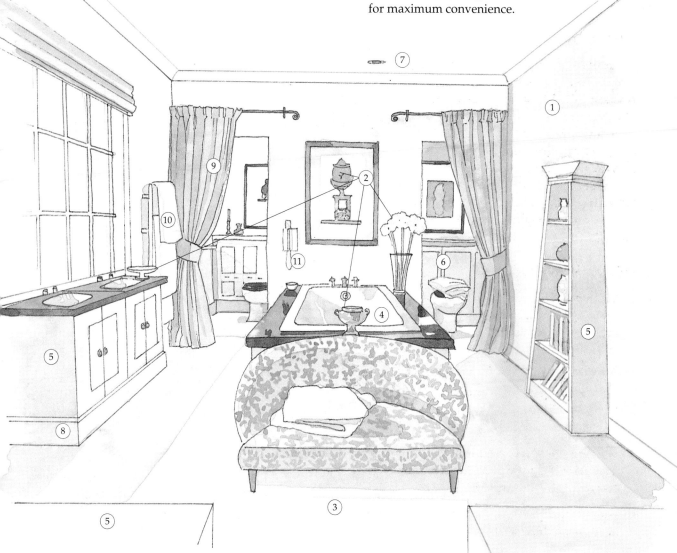

Clean lines distinguish this modern stylish bathroom scheme in black, grey and white relieved by vivid yellow.

Family Bathroom

They may be queuing to get in, but are you sure this is as an indication of the attractiveness of your family bathroom? Might it not simply mean that your home could really do with additional facilities?

It may be a long time since we had to make do with a tub before the fire and a hut in the garden, but it seems that we are slow to recognize the vital role a bathroom plays in the smooth running of family life and it is only now that houses are being constructed with bathrooms matching bedrooms something like *pro rata*. A recent survey by house builders has revealed the somewhat unsurprising information that what most appeals to the current house-buying public are big kitchens and 'lots of bathrooms'.

When it comes to planning a new bathroom or refurbishing an old one, the criteria that apply to bathrooms in general (see page 82) apply especially to the family bathroom. In addition there is a need for even more stringent safety precautions in view of the wide range of ages likely to be using this bathroom. A lockable cupboard for the storage of medicines is useful and an out-of-the-way space will be needed for storing caustic cleaning materials if the household contains young children. Locks on windows and the elimination of sharp corners in the bathroom will also help maintain safety. Non-slip surfaces should be incorporated wherever sensible and grab rails are a useful addition if there is an elderly person in the house. Taps need to be chosen carefully: they should be easily manipulated, even with wet hands. A mixer-tap system will help prevent bathroom users from being exposed to extremes of temperature and, incidentally, will make for easier hair washing.

The furnishing of the family bathroom will depend very much upon the size of room at your disposal. As it is likely that the bathroom may be occupied by more than one person at a time, keeping the room as clear as possible (especially around the bath) will be a priority. Twin wash basins housed in a built-in unit are ideal and, if space allows, a separate shower could prove an invaluable alternative bathing facility. A chair or stool (possibly with a lift-up seat and storage below) will give you somewhere to sit or lay down clothes as well as providing a surface for a small child to stand on when reaching a basin. Privacy is often a sensitive subject with growing children and if you can provide some minimal form of screening around the WC (a low projecting wall, a screen or curtains will suffice), this will do much to help. If possible, a separate WC should also be available for when the bathroom is occupied. It is not possible to over-estimate how long a teenager will spend in the bathroom!

The best decorations for a family bathroom are simple, bright and cheerful (some children may need encouragement to enter!). If the bathroom is for use by both adults and children, try to avoid deliberately childish themes, especially in any permanent fixtures (you, and your children when they are older, might regret those teddy-bear tiles). One idea, though, would be to introduce a younger theme in a replaceable shower curtain. Buy a fabric of your choice and line this with a plain plastic lining. However, by choosing a seashore, nautical or botanical theme, you might well suit all tastes. Surfaces, if they are to remain looking good, will need to be resilient. Ceramic tiles or a paint finish (with stencilling, if you like) are best for walls and sheet vinyl is probably the most serviceable covering for the floor. An easily removed, non-absorptive carpet might also be considered.

Useful extras for the bathroom would be plenty of mirrors, as large a heated towel rail as you can accommodate – there is little so uncomforting as a damp towel – and a wall-mounted hair dryer located near a mirror (but away from sources of water).

HOW THE ROOM MIGHT LOOK

THE PLAN

Space is not a problem in this good-looking bathroom, planned for adults and older children. A pleasant view is assured from the bath by positioning it under the window. The WC and shower are separated from the body of the room by a low wall and the provision of a separate shower and double sinks allows for the bathroom to be occupied by more than one person at a time.

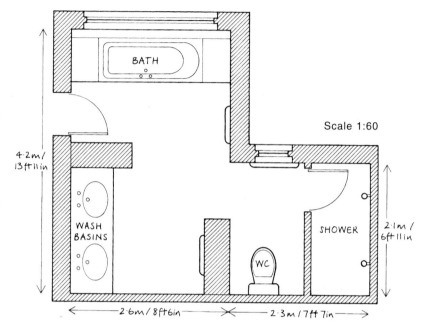

DESIGN DECISIONS

1 Scheme Clean and crisp, this sharp scheme combines black, grey and white with bright yellow. The whole is softened by the introduction of green foliage.

2 Walls Pale grey and black tiles provide a good wall protection while being aesthetically pleasing and bringing a sparkle to the room.

3 Flooring Made to withstand drenching, polished marble tiles are easy to maintain.

4 Lighting Utilitarian safety lamps in this context take on a stylish look. Light-coloured reflective walls mean that rather less light is needed than in a room with dark matt surfaces.

5 Wash basins Side-by-side double basins are practical when bathroom facilities are in demand.

AN ALTERNATIVE BATHROOM

THE PLAN

Roof space has been reclaimed to form this bathroom for the exclusive use of junior family members. The floor level steps up to leave a void for essential plumbing while at the same time creating some additional interest.

Primary colours form the basis of the scheme for this bathroom dedicated to the younger members of a family.

DESIGN DECISIONS

Scheme Primary colours ensure that this bathroom always offers a bright welcome to entice possibly reluctant bathers.

Walls White ceramic tiles are applied to the lower portion of the walls to take 'the worst of the wet'. The choice of a wallpaper with a similar white back-ground successfully distracts the eye from an uneven ceiling line.

Bath The round shape and blue colour of the bath give all the appearance of a paddling pool, inviting youngsters to jump in. The setting of the bath provides two sides for maximum access and allows an adult to reach bathing children easily.

Wash basins Double basins are always useful where multiple occupancy is envisaged.

Mats These are placed near to the WC, bath and basins to help prevent carpet damage.

CHILDREN'S ROOMS

I need my own space' is a familiar cry of the late twentieth century. But very rarely do we relate this lament to our children's lives. We are so often tempted to relegate them to the smallest rooms (where there is, in theory, less room to make a mess) and somehow we don't imagine that their little lives could possibly be so full of confusion and clutter as to require a well-thought-out, organized, private space all to themselves. We forget about the pressures brought on by bickering brothers and sisters, the claustrophobic life of the school room and the confrontations of a competitive playground, not to mention the constant attention of parents who 'don't understand'. If children are to survive and to develop into sane adulthood, they need all the help we can give them and if, by allocating them their own special quiet space, we can help this along, then so much the better.

The thought process needed for the planning of children's rooms is very similar to that required for the other rooms in a house. First naturally come the practicalities: the activities to cater for, the storage to accommodate and comfort and security to attend to. Then there are the aesthetic considerations – also very important. Who, for instance, cannot recall the wallpaper of their room of formative years? So pause a moment to think before reaching for that book of clown wallpaper prints. Careful planning before you start decorating will ensure that your child will be safe, comfortable and happy.

What activities is your child likely to perform in his/her room? To name but a few – sleeping, eating, playing, craftwork, study and, last but not least, entertaining. It is a good idea to create separate areas for each activity so that the child who may spend many hours in this one room has some contrast between the different activities and so that 'messy' areas do not intrude into other parts of the room – though this, of course, will depend upon the space available. If two are to share one room, efforts should be made to allocate specific areas for each child which 'belong' to him/her and for which he/she is responsible. This will help to encourage growing children to feel more responsible for their room in the future.

The planning of children's rooms does differ from other rooms in two important regards. First, whatever materials you select for your scheme are likely to be severely tested. Water may be splashed, food dropped and wall surfaces scuffed, so your choice of finishes and fabrics will have to be very carefully considered and their ability to stand up to wear and tear must be a priority. Second, children have a habit of growing up very fast and at each stage they seem to develop an allergic reaction to the scheme that just a couple of years ago was deemed so appropriate. Durability and adaptability are therefore the keys to satisfying the young person's growing requirements and evolving taste.

The safety provisions required will to some extent depend upon the age of the child. But whatever his/her age, the danger points to pay particular attention to are: any electrical installations (sockets, switches, wires and so on); light fittings (these may be knocked over or skin burnt on an exposed bulb); heating appliances (with their danger of scalding or setting fires) and windows. Security glass in a window will help and good locking devices are a must, but grilles need to be considered in the context of a fire outbreak (that is, they must be easily removed in an emergency). Attention should also be

There's no need for story books to prime a child's imagination in this charming 'underwater' bedroom.

given to the choice of furniture. This should be stable, of a suitable size, without sharp corners or rough surfaces, and be made of a non-shattering material. Care should also be taken to avoid the use of paints containing lead.

Cleanliness and hygiene have a high priority – especially where the small baby is concerned. Scrubbable surfaces and the avoidance of crannies where dirt may lurk will help, as will the use of washable materials.

SURFACES

Children will be children – and to expect them to have the same reverence for your home as you have is a tall order! Rather than installing vulnerable surfaces, tough resilient finishes will give you more peace of mind and your child greater freedom. Hard, splinter-free flooring in a young baby's room may prove the best solution. Area rugs (non-slip) to give a feeling of comfort can be added, and later a fitted carpet installed once the child has left the 'messy

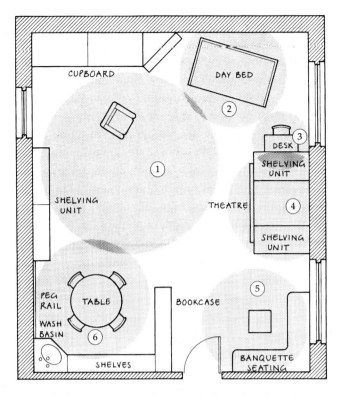

*Activity zoning in a playroom. 1: floor play, 2: resting,
3: writing, 4: play acting, 5: quiet reading,
6: craftwork and eating*

years' behind him/her. When it comes to walls, cute wallpapers, attractive as they may be, do not necessarily provide the ideal finish. Paint surfaces, on the other hand, are easily cleaned, can be renewed without too much trouble and form a great background for both baby effects and the older child's posters. The focus of many a non-sleeping hour, ceilings are frequently neglected: they offer the most wonderful opportunity to fill your child's mind with the material of sweet dreams – of the Man-in-the-moon, Superman or Peter Pan.

FURNISHINGS

Whether or not to scale furniture to the size of the child is a personal decision. Although child-sized furniture may offer greater comfort and safety to the young child, it will inevitably be outgrown in a very

Pine pieces against a plain background do all the decorating that is necessary in this back-to-nature children's sitting room.

short time. Perhaps a mix of miniature and full-sized furnishings (which will stay with the child through later years) may be the best solution. Seating for the visiting adult should not be forgotten.

STORAGE

With all the activities likely to be undertaken in this room come the inevitable paraphernalia and resulting storage problems. Forward planning in this area will mean that the child has few excuses for untidiness and unsuitable items are not left out for him/her to misuse (ten minutes with a tin of baby powder and a child can make quite an impression on a room!). It is recommended that some hidden storage (behind doors, screens, in bags and so on) is provided for a quick tidy-away, while other areas are left open for the display of favourite toys and books.

A peg rail is a useful addition to storage facilities.

LIGHTING

Safety cannot be overemphasized where lighting is concerned. Although many table lamps are attractively designed for use in children's rooms, these should always be carefully positioned, out of reach of the young child, and trailing cables should be avoided. Good overhead or wall lighting is what is needed, but care should be taken to ensure that the resting child is not blinded by the glare from an unshielded bulb. A glowing night light kept on till morning offers much reassurance to a young child when nightmares loom. Although few electric sockets may be required for the very young baby, remember to install sufficient for future needs as he/she grows up. These can be blanked off until required.

Baby Nursery

Anticipating the arrival of a new baby can be such an exciting time and the temptation to concentrate on the pretty details of the nursery decoration hard to resist. However, if your baby is to be healthy, comfortable and safe, it is essential that adequate thought be given to some practical elements before anything else.

Safety must always be the first consideration – see the introductory section to this chapter for guidance. In addition it should be remembered that the small immobile bundle of joy will, in a matter of months, double in size and will attain a high degree of mobility, not to mention curiosity. Although few electrical sockets will be required in the nursery at this stage, they should be planned for with an eye to the future and those not currently required can be blanked off until needed.

Temperature is an important factor for the comfort of your baby. Controllable central-heating radiators are probably the most successful way of safely heating a child's room, but these should be out of reach if possible, either hidden behind an item of furniture or protected by a guard. It is often forgotten that a young baby is just as vulnerable to overheating as to the cold. For this reason it is important to provide adequate ventilation (at a safe height) and to ensure that a baby's cot is positioned well away from any direct source of heat.

A wash basin with running water in a nursery is often considered a luxury, but when it is seen in the context of the lifetime of the room, the benefits become more evident. The nursery may soon become the child's playroom, then a teenager's bedroom. Finally it may even become a guest room. In each of these guises the inclusion of a wash basin could be considered a bonus. If the basin is housed within a vanity unit, shelves beneath can be used at this first

A prime example of a nursery achieved at minimal expense and with future adaptability firmly in mind.

stage for the storage of the baby's necessities and later perhaps for storing toys.

Few items of furniture are needed in the nursery of a very young baby. A cot, chest of drawers (the top of which, when covered with padding, could be used for changing the baby) and an easy chair with low arms for the nursing mother are all that are required. Shelves for displaying pictures, toys and books help to decorate the room. A trolley to house the baby's nappies, cream, powder, a bucket and so on is a useful addition and can be put to other use when no longer required in the nursery. Later on, as the baby develops, a small wardrobe, high chair and play pen might be purchased.

The decoration of the nursery need not involve great expense. Plain painted walls that allow for surface decorations to be added and changed as the child matures are a good idea. Pictures, stencils,

mobiles, paper borders and pasted cutouts are all decorations that will inspire the imagination of your child. Colours should be bright and cheerful, and in these enlightened times there is no need to be restrained by the 'blue for a boy, pink for a girl' dictum.

When it comes to floors, hygiene, ease of maintenance and the child's comfort and safety can all be served by laying such materials as cushioned vinyl, cork or hard wood (so long as it is splinterless). The addition of easily washed play mats will soften the hard floor effect.

It is preferable for curtains not to drop to the floor as these may well be used by the child to support himself/herself. The addition of a blackout blind or curtain lining may help your child to sleep in the early evening and will help prevent him/her awakening with the dawn.

How the room might look

THE PLAN

The layout is extremely simple and yet caters for all the needs of a new-born child. Storage is provided by a free-standing chest, and shelving units attached to the right-hand wall. The shelves have been cleverly designed, leaving a space where a cot might be sited at a later date. Seating in front of the window allows mother to cradle her child in comfort and to enjoy the view. A second chair is for guests or for laying out clothes for the following day. The room remains uncluttered – essential for the baby who will soon be crawling.

DESIGN DECISIONS

1 **Scheme** Sunshine yellow is contrasted with navy blue to give this room a bright cheerful feel suitable for either male or female offspring.

2 **Walls** Softly stippled, washable paintwork is easily cleaned and provides a perfect background for childhood decorations.

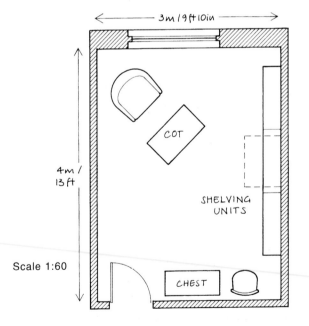

3 **Paper frieze** This charming animal border handsomely decorates the walls and can be easily changed for one with a more mature theme when the child is older.

4 Flooring Wood veneer planks sealed with a coating of vinyl are both practical and attractive. It can be treated as any other vinyl flooring and upkeep is minimal.

5 Easy chair Bought second-hand and painted smart navy, this Lloyd loom chair with its comfortable cushion and low arms is perfect for the nursing mother.

6 Shelving system Basic in conception and execution, these beautifully dressed shelves are securely attached to the wall and will easily adapt for the child's future needs. The choice of navy-striped fabric to enclose them is inspired – smart and yet not tying the room to babyhood.

7 Storage baskets Ideal for all baby's kit, they can be removed for easy access and transported to laundry or car.

8 Changing table An essential item, this one is cantilevered off the wall at a convenient height and its colour co-ordinates well with the chosen scheme.

9 Window A lever operates the opening of the top windows to provide ventilation without placing the baby in a draught. A blind will cut out the light when required.

10 Radiator Currently exposed, this can easily be enclosed once the child is mobile.

11 Mobile A decorative feature, strategically placed for baby's amusement.

12 Electrical socket Well hidden in an unobtrusive corner, this is blanked off anticipating a toddler's curiosity.

Pre-school Playroom

Anyone who has cared for children of between the ages of one and five years knows all too well just what are the important things to remember when planning a playroom. For a mother to remain relaxed about her child spending time in this room, supervised or unsupervised, she needs to know that the child cannot damage himself/herself or the room and that he/she will be entertained for a reasonable length of time. It is also important that, after playtime, the process of cleaning up can be carried out with the minimum of effort, mother and child both having better things to occupy them. At this age of maximum mobility and minimum attention span these are tough demands.

A gate as well as a door at the entrance will help ensure that the child is contained within the room and within earshot when mother's back is turned. To lessen noise from the playroom, install plenty of soft finishes within the room.

The creation of zones for different activities will help punctuate the child's day as he/she moves from one activity to another, and will help with the organization of storage associated with each occupation. For example, in one corner a table and chairs might be positioned on plastic sheeting to protect the flooring and craft materials stored nearby. Other areas might be dedicated to eating, quiet story-telling, play-acting, resting and so on.

To enable you to keep the room in reasonable order, plenty of storage facilities will be needed. In general these are best housed in fitted units – apart from them being more stable and less likely to trap tiny fingers, such units will give the room a neater finish. A blackboard might be attached to the front of one, a pinboard to another, and perhaps a third might carry a plastic mirror. Any free-standing units, so long as they are well weighted, could be used to divide areas within the room. Additional storage could be provided in chests, in boxes on castors, in baskets or even in a hammock (especially if this were

to fit in with the theme of your room – for instance, 'Treasure Island'). If the child is also to use the room for sleeping, a bed and some kind of wardrobe will, of course, be needed. Although initially a child might not need hanging space, it is wise to allow for this as he/she will soon be into clothing that will require more than just shelves. A really useful tip for a playroom is to fix a peg rail with hooks, as found in Shaker homes, at dado-rail height (90cm/3ft). This could be used for hanging clothing, small chairs or drawstring bags of favourite toys, or for displaying decorative items.

As children mature they need the company of others to develop their social skills fully, and so it is important to make provision for visiting friends. A small table with several chairs where they can gather is a good idea – useful for both play and meal times. And as children seem to simply love to stay over, you might consider bunk beds or some other novel sleeping solution.

The decoration of a playroom can be great fun – you'll be amazed at what can be achieved with a staple gun, a few metres of fabric, some pots of paint, several sheets of MDF and a fertile imagination. Create your own circus tent, underwater world or Indian camp! An alternative approach would be not to have a specific theme in mind but to use strong bright colours as a background for constantly changing visual shows. These temporary decorations could be attached to walls by means of removable adhesive, mobiles could be hung from the ceiling and prints suspended from a picture rail. To help develop your child's taste ask him/her to make selections from a range of ideas you deem suitable.

In this bright and cheerful playroom, walls have been kept plain so as to permit surface decorations to change and to allow for the room to grow with the child.

How the room might look

THE PLAN

The furniture in this well-organized playroom has been zoned to allow for areas of different activity. A theatre divides a drawing/writing area from a quiet story-telling corner with banquette seating (plus storage beneath the seats) and a low bookcase encloses a craft/dining area. A shelving unit for display, a day bed and full-height storage cupboard complete the furnishings.

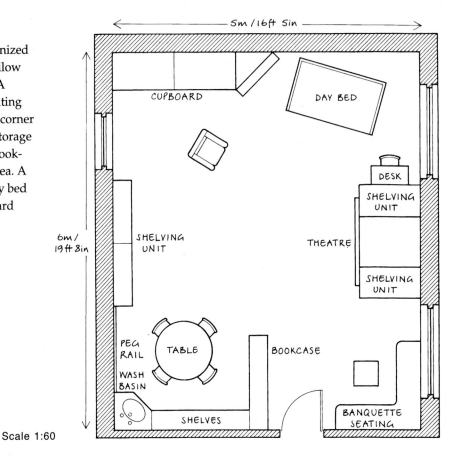

Scale 1:60

DESIGN DECISIONS

1 **Scheme** The simplest of painted walls form an uncluttered backdrop for primary-coloured furnishings and toys. In this south-facing room the cool blue is compensated for by the warm natural light entering from the two large windows.

2 **Animal theme** Represented by the picture on the wall and echoed in the cushions, soft toys, window blinds and floor mat.

3 **Flooring** A polished wooden plank floor is easy to maintain and warm in feel. A mat is provided for when a 'soft landing' is required.

4 **Furniture** The blond wood of the floor is reflected in the finish to several items of furniture.

5 **Day bed** This doubles up as a cot for the young child to sleep in. When the child is older, it can be converted to a bed.

6 **Cupboard** A full-height fitted cupboard provides masses of storage. Later a hanging rail can be fitted to take the growing child's clothes.

7 **Desk** This extends from one of the tall, wall-fixed units and is bathed in natural light from the nearby window.

8 Table and four chairs This grouping forms an assembly point for meals and play. Proportioned for little people, the table has a polished wood surface varnished with clear protective lacquer.

9 Theatre Two tall wall-fixed units combine with a theatre front to form a secret space where plays can be performed.

10 Building blocks Giant foam 'bricks' are light and safe to use. They help to develop the child's creative abilities and to exercise young muscles. When not constructing, the child can use the blocks as seats.

11 Lighting In a co-ordinating style, this pendant light can be adjusted so that it is always out of the growing child's reach. Similar lights focus on the craft table and the reading area.

12 Blackboard Children will always be tempted to scribble on walls, so why not provide a special surface for the purpose? The pedimented shape of the board echoes that of the theatre and the building blocks.

Teenager's Den

You may be lucky enough to have a perfectly behaved teenager living in your home or you may belong to one of the millions of families with typical, slightly out-of-control offspring. The teenager will probably want to make too much noise, be unlikely to see the merits of being tidy and have ideas on decoration that involve sticking things other than wallpaper on walls. He/she may well develop into a proud home owner in the future, but meanwhile, accepting that 'teenagers will be teenagers' will go a long way towards harmonious living in the home you share with a child-adult going through a prolonged youth crisis.

Deciding upon just how much isolation each of you wants or thinks is desirable is a matter for negotiation and the outcome will probably determine which room in the house is selected for the teenager's room. A converted loft or basement could provide an ideal self-contained space where neither party's life impinges too greatly on the other – a place where friends can be entertained, noise made and privacy maintained.

The teenager's involvement in deciding upon the decoration of the room is very important if he/she is to have any respect for his/her surroundings and if he/she is to be encouraged to maintain them well. Teenage years are a great time for experimentation and, although mistakes will surely be made, it is hoped that lessons will also be learned. An interior designer specializing in young people's rooms has been quoted as saying: 'Ask them what they want, then bargain!' This seems a fairly sensible approach to adopt.

As in the younger child's playroom, it is a good idea to create zones for different activities within the teenager's den. In the sleeping area, duvets are an easy solution to bed-making and you may wish to make provisions for friends staying overnight – say, bunk beds or a day bed that can also be used for seating during the day. Hammocks strung across the beams in a loft ceiling are a fun idea for the teenager with frequent guests.

An ideal study area would be located in the vicinity of a good source of natural light and would have a number of electrical sockets positioned nearby. Space for a work surface, a bookcase and housing for computer equipment should be allowed for. A flexible storage unit is also a good idea for accommodating a television and audio equipment.

The provision of personal bathing facilities within the room itself will free more bathroom time for the rest of the family. Most teenagers seem to prefer a shower to a bath and, as this is more economical and takes up less space, the idea could be encouraged. A cubicle might be housed within a wall of deep cupboards or in a small room annexe.

Sometimes it seems as though teenagers think of little else apart from their clothes, so a dressing space will be an important area of the room. A walk-in closet is ideal: it provides lots of space and can be shut out of view at will. Alternatively large cupboards with masses of hanging space and a full-length mirror could be provided. A system of wire baskets within a metal framework works well for the quick 'filing' of items of clothing within a cupboard, and a rail on castors behind a curtain makes a cheap wardrobe substitute.

Decoration ideas are soon outgrown, so a flexible scheme is likely to be the most successful. Plain walls of an oil-based paint will provide a good background on to which posters and so on can be attached (and replaced when no longer in favour) and non-themed soft-furnishing fabrics will give the room decor longevity. A carpet with thick underlay will help to prevent noise pollution.

*Bright primary colours add a punch to this fun teenager's
room in cool grey.*

How the room might look

THE PLAN

Flexibility is the key to this teenager's den. All furniture is free-standing and, when outgrown, the sturdy DIY climbing-frame structure can be redesigned and repositioned with little effort. The desk, providing ample space for two to work, sits neatly beneath a storage deck that can easily be converted to a spare bed when required. Additional storage is provided in the two cupboards, and an audio system is to be found in a low unit beside a sofa.

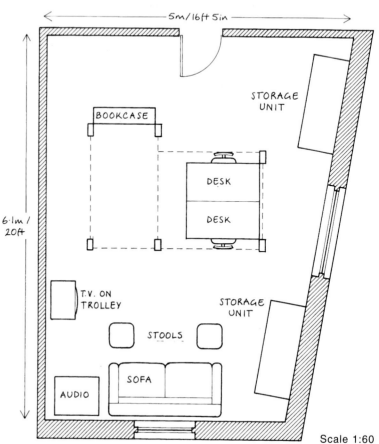

Scale 1:60

DESIGN DECISIONS

1   **Scheme** Bright primary colours are used to enliven the essentially neutral backdrop. Black unit fronts and bed covers punctuate the scheme.

2   **Walls** Paint of the palest grey gives this room a clean, uncluttered look and forms a good background for pictures and posters. The teenager is unlikely to tire of this plain treatment and can change the look with the minimum of cost and effort by simply swapping pictures.

3   **Flooring** Polished floorboards provide a flooring that is practical without appearing utilitarian, and forms a natural link with the climbing frame. A grey carpet, continued from the landing, gives the central area a softer feel.

4   **Climbing frame** Constructed from pine, this is an adaptable structure to provide amusement and accommodation for two teenagers – with a possible space for a third to stay over. The frame also helps to enclose the study area.

5   **Storage cupboards** Positioned to either side of the window and in the same style as the desks, these units are cleverly divided into display shelves, large pull-out drawers and a hanging cupboard – addressing all the needs of the teenager.

6   **Desks** With ample workspace for two, a pair of desks with lockable cupboards provide the centre-piece for this perfect study area. A generous waste-bin beneath asks to be filled!

7 Window treatment Venetian fine blinds, sitting within window reveals, create a tailored look and allow the occupants easy control of the amount of natural light entering the room.

8 Lighting Practical and fun, the various fittings have been chosen to amuse and to target light where needed. The fittings are free-standing and can easily be repositioned should the furniture arrangement change.

9 Coloured boxes These robust containers are roomy and good-looking. Out of the way on top of the cupboards, they provide extra long-term storage space.

10 Door furniture and light switches These are white and modern in design to co-ordinate with this contemporary interior.

WORKROOMS

The world has evolved considerably since the days when the only workrooms within the home were considered to be 'his study' or 'his workshop'. It was uncertain just how much work was undertaken in these rooms, but their attractions appeared to increase as domestic pressures mounted!

Today the spheres of work, study and leisure frequently merge. Many more women have taken up employment in recent years and family commitments mean that, in many cases, the home has become the most suitable location for work. Technology too has played its part, enabling information to be swapped from remote locations and rendering commuting to the city office an obsolete practice for many. Technology has also meant that domestic chores are reduced, thus freeing many more hours for leisure pursuits.

The rewards of combining work and leisure in the home are numerous and, by now, well recognized. A work package that includes spending the day in close proximity to loved ones, the elimination of wasted travel time and the possibility of working in an altogether more pleasant environment is indeed attractive.

It is not necessary, nor is it always practical, to devote a large space or considerable budget to providing a work area – it may even be self-defeating if the income gained through employment is eroded by the cost of providing facilities and if the space sacrificed detracts from family life. Perhaps just an old door supported by two second-hand filing cabinets (which will double up as a dressing table, see page 112) in the spare room are all that is needed. It is really just a question of priorities. However, one thing we are sure of is that a room that is properly equipped, well located and appropriately decorated is more conducive to work than one that has to serve other purposes as well.

It is not long since out-buildings were thought of as a liability rather than the asset they are now considered to be. These form ideal locations for workrooms, but if they are in short supply, room must be found for a workspace within the home itself. For preference and convenience this should be a dedicated space – possibly a converted basement or loft? Or perhaps an extension could be constructed or a teenager's abandoned bedroom refurbished? A room dedicated to work will allow for peace and privacy and will mean that work and equipment can be left out until next required. It also allows you to decorate the room in a workmanlike fashion to encourage concentration.

If, however, it is not possible to dedicate a whole room to work, much thought needs to be applied towards ensuring that any multi-purpose room does not compromise both work and leisure activities and that the two functions do not become confused. To divide a room into distinct play and work zones, a piece of useful furniture (such as a bookcase) could be placed to form a screen, or perhaps the two areas could be defined by a change in floor level.

Although you are primarily creating a workroom, do not neglect to provide for some relaxation. Without the natural punctuations of a day in a busy city office, time can seem to drag. When these moments arrive, it is often better to switch off completely for a short period and then return to your work refreshed. An easy chair, music, hot/cold drinks, reading matter – these will all help to provide a contrast to the main activity.

Bookshelves and a desk make good use of this understairs space and natural light is enhanced by the inclusion of a mirror.

STORAGE

Try to plan storage right from the start rather than let it evolve haphazardly. By all means reuse existing furniture, but wherever possible custom-make and build in for a more streamlined, organized, efficient appearance.

LIGHTING

Although sited in a workspace, lighting does not have to be utilitarian so long as it fulfils its purpose. Concentrate on providing a good overall level of illumination and ensuring that specific tasks are in good glare-free light coming from the correct direction.

Unlined ecru silk-taffeta curtains, slotted on to a clear acrylic pole, demonstrate David Hicks' innovative approach to window dressing in this smart study area.

Home Office

The great technology revolution of the latter part of the twentieth century has impacted upon our lives in no less a way than the industrial revolution on the lives of the people in the mid-nineteenth century. All the commuting, the monolithic head office, the secretaries, the separation from home and family – these embedded life threads are gradually being consigned to the history books. Our concerns for quality of air, of work time and of family life have ensured their demise.

The home office, for many, provides the perfect solution. It permits you to work variable hours to suit your lifestyle and that of your family in agreeable surroundings and ensures that little time is wasted on travel.

Your home working area can adopt many guises depending upon the type of work undertaken and the space available. Whatever the set-up, your office should offer you the easiest possible method of working. With the working week averaging some forty hours, it is clearly worth spending some time on planning the space where it is going to take place.

Distractions in the home can come from many directions – interruptions from family members, demands created by other activities happening in the same space, callers at the door and so on. For your office to be productive in these circumstances, you will need to isolate yourself to some extent from what is going on around you. This may involve housing the office in a separate building, attaching locks to the door, installing separate telephone lines or even building in some form of soundproofing.

The professional home office should reek of efficiency. Not only will this impress the visiting bank manager, business colleagues, representatives and clients, but it will also help you make the transition from domestic to work mode so much more easily. This atmosphere can best be engendered by creating

Natural light floods into this businesslike loft office space.

a dedicated work area which is furnished to match and which is not used for any other purpose. The ideal office has its own entrance and cloakroom nearby. Coffee-making facilities and comfortable seating for guests are an added bonus.

Decorations should generally tend towards the more serious colours (neutrals and deeps being particularly suitable) and distracting patterns used with caution. Many suitable floorings are available and selection will most probably be determined by budget. Cord carpets are reasonably priced; they are hard-wearing and will not be easily damaged by chair castors (less hard-wearing floorings can be protected by clear plastic mats positioned beneath desk chairs). Soft furnishings are best kept restrained – simple clean lines and discreet trims to give a tailored finish. Should funds be limited, a basic cloth such as ticking, made up with trims of petersham ribbon, could be used to great effect.

Lighting needs to be well targeted and care should be taken to ensure that glare is not caused by the reflection of light fittings on a computer screen. Remember also to light storage areas and bookshelves. To make best use of any available daylight, site desks directly in front of windows (ensuring that these are screened in some way if the view beyond is likely to cause a distraction).

It may be tempting, in this domestic environment, to incorporate residential furnishings. These will certainly make the office appear more homely, but for comfort and efficiency, purpose-made office furniture is recommended. A computer stand on castors to house monitor, keyboard, printer, paper and so on is ideal and will accommodate all these items at the right height. Your chair is equally, if not more, important. This should be well made, ergonomically designed and adjustable so that your sitting position is not injurious to your posture.

Nothing detracts more from the appearance of an office than for every surface to be spilling over with paperwork, files and samples. Far from it promoting an image of endeavour, it demonstrates that the owner is disorganized and consequently inefficient. This problem can be overcome by the provision of sufficient, conveniently placed and well-designed storage space. Storage units can, of course, be in the form of free-standing cupboards and shelves, but look much neater and more streamlined if built in. Should the room already contain fitted wardrobes, the interiors of these could be converted: the rails could be replaced with suitable partitioning or, if the room is to be reused as a bedroom in the future, perhaps a free-standing framework could be incorporated into the wardrobe.

It may be that you are not professionally employed, yet still need some sort of management centre to run your personal life and an active household efficiently. This office could well be based upon

nothing more than a telephone and a file, and finding a suitable location should not cause a problem. The bay window of a bedroom, the space in the hallway under the stairs, a desk in the library, a recess in the dining room, a cupboard in a rarely used guest room – these may all be capable of housing a mini office.

Much can be done to disguise work and storage elements in a multi-functional room. Files can be bound in attractive wallpaper, a trestle table can be draped with a full-length cloth that co-ordinates with your room scheme and which conceals beneath it your work paraphernalia, and pinboards can be made of attractive material trellised with some pretty ribbons.

As an alternative to making your work accessories good to look at, you might consider concealing your whole work area within a cupboard, behind a screen or masked from view behind a curtain or blind.

How the room might look

THE PLAN

Loft space has been converted to create a spacious room for business activities. The structural contours provide architectural interest and roof lights allow natural light to flood in. The furnishings have been cunningly arranged so as not to waste space where headroom is limited. To one side desks are lined up under the natural light and opposite a relaxed seating/sleeping area is arranged. Bookshelves are contained within a triangular recess and at the opposite end of the room an area is partitioned off for storage of equipment, files and stationery.

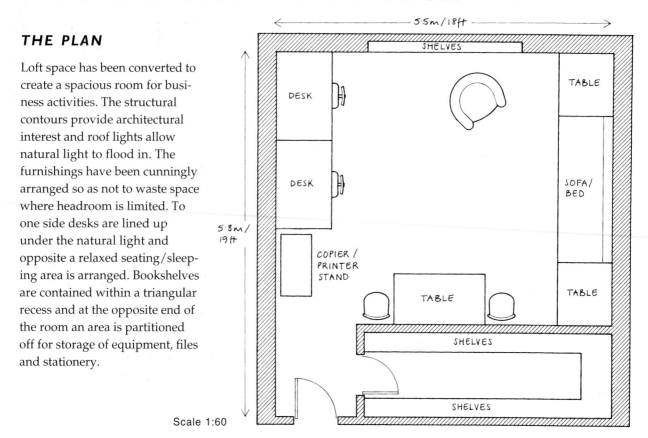

Scale 1:60

DESIGN DECISIONS

1 **Scheme** White walls and beige flooring combine to form the background to modern black furnishings in this loft space: a very businesslike scheme, relieved only by a scattering of brightly coloured chintz cushions.

2 **Desks** These are of a good size and have additional pull-out surfaces. Faced with laminate, they are tough and easily cleaned.

3 **Bookshelves** A case of a storage problem becoming a decorative feature: the triangular shape of the recess adds interest to a featureless wall.

4 **Sofa** In the seating area, a day bed has been formed by placing a foam mattress on a solid base. A bolster and numerous other cushions give the bed its day-time disguise.

5 **Lighting** Large black Anglepoise lamps are of an appropriate style to go with the scheme and to direct light exactly where needed. Table lamps would be a suitable choice in a more domestic style of office. Natural light from dormer windows and a skylight floods the room.

6 **Flooring** A low-pile corded carpet is suitably robust to stand up to chair casters and heavy usage.

Studio/Workshop

The dream of most creative people, a studio is a wonderful space in which to indulge the imagination, a peaceful oasis where artistic endeavours are nurtured. Whatever your passion – dance or découpage, photography or physiotherapy, cake-making or calligraphy – a dedicated, well-equipped studio provides the ideal environment for its expression.

Choosing the right location for your studio/workshop is critical if home and work are to operate harmoniously side by side. As with the other work areas discussed in this book, a certain amount of separation from the rest of the home and its activities may be desirable – except, of course, where there is a need to be within view or earshot of children or an elderly family member. As well as the hazard of home life impinging upon this creative space, there is the reverse problem of the studio perhaps causing a problem for the rest of the household. Your pastime/work may involve unsociable elements such as noise and mess that will require some form of isolation if they are not to upset other household members.

When thinking of creating a workshop space, it is a great idea first to make a list of all the activities your work involves, because from that list will evolve all else that you are likely to need (see the introductory section to this chapter, page 112).

The availability of services may well determine where your studio or workshop is best located. Here are some of the facilities you might require:

▶ **Power points** For tools, audio equipment, heating, cooking, lighting, refrigeration and so on. As always, it is wise to think ahead and build in more sockets than you currently require, remembering to site these where most convenient (possibly at worktop height).

▶ **Water** For photographic work, pottery, painting, cooking, cleaning up and so on.

Consider whether you need a hot water supply as well as cold. Mixer taps with a single spout that can be swung to one side over a large sink will allow you to run water to the desired temperature and to manoeuvre a bucket in and out of the sink easily.

▶ **Gas** For firing, heating, welding and so on. If a mains supply is not available, it may be worthwhile considering a tank supply.

▶ **Ventilation** To eliminate any noxious fumes/smells and to maintain a suitable temperature in which to work. This can be provided by an open window or fan system (either manually or automatically operated).

▶ **Lighting** For all your tasks and for overall conditions – think carefully about what sort of lighting would best suit your purposes. It is always advisable to include some free-standing lighting that can be directed at will – for instance, an Anglepoise lamp. Fluorescent fittings provide good overall shadowless lighting, but be careful with your selection of bulbs if you have a need to recreate daylight conditions (for colour rendition purposes and so on).

▶ **Security** Door locks to keep your studio equipment and work safe, and to exclude minors from dangerous areas. You may require a safe for storing precious materials and an alarm system to reinforce your security. Always keep poisonous substances under lock and key. Where there is a fire hazard, smoke alarms should be installed and emergency fire-fighting equipment kept close at hand.

Red and white combine to provide a bright and cheerful workroom on a budget.

The clever planning of storage facilities within your workshop will be vital to its success. If you apply the same principles as used in planning kitchen storage, you will be on the right track. Plan chests, filing cupboards and similar units are best designed to your own specification and, wherever possible, built in and out of the way. A distinction should be made between those items you may be using on a daily basis and those used less frequently. You may choose to store often-used tools on a wall-mounted racking system where they can be easily reached, while those that are rarely required can be housed within less accessible units.

The position, size and height of work surfaces should also be carefully thought out. The availability of natural light will probably determine the best site for your working zone and it is important to remember that, for your comfort and health, your seating arrangement should be ergonomically determined.

When it comes to deciding upon finishes for the various surfaces within your studio, consider first the practicalities. What will stand up to the 'abuse' you are likely to inflict? A painted cement floor (which can easily be repainted when badly damaged) is suit-able for heavy-duty wear and areas where high temperatures are involved. A sheet-vinyl or ceramic-tile flooring may be the answer for messy but less damaging activities. For 'dry' activities, cork or vinyl tiles (which, when worn out, can be individually replaced) may be the most suitable floor covering. If you are working with textiles, a hard floor will be easier than a soft one to keep clean. A wooden flooring may prove the most apt for a room used for physical activities, but do take care with slipperiness and splinters. Whatever your selection, think also about the acoustics of the room (soft finishes help to cushion sound), and remember that, where mess is concerned, a threshold mat will help prevent dirt permeating your home. Walls with a gloss-paint finish are generally considered fairly robust, and can be repainted when badly scarred.

Your second consideration should be the aesthetics. For most situations a plain paint wall surface may provide the best answer. It will form an ideal blank canvas against which your activities can take place and can act as a display surface to which items can be attached with removable masking tape or adhesive pads. A picture rail might also prove useful.

How the room might look

THE PLAN

Eked out of a larger workshop space, this inviting corner caters for the multi-purpose craftsperson. Storage and workspace are the priorities in this studio converted on a budget.

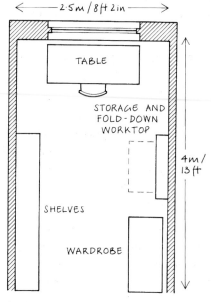

Scale 1:60

DESIGN DECISIONS

1 **Scheme** White gloss paint has been used to good effect visually to enlarge this restricted space. Red introduces a sense of fun to the straightforward two-colour scheme.

2 **Flooring** Sheet vinyl in white with a red diagonal stripe reflects the light, is a dream to clean and is inexpensive.

3 **Shelving** Of the most basic kind, these shelves are deep and well supported. Notice how the upper shelf has an upstand at its edge to prevent rolls of paper from falling off. Hooks on the wall below allow vacuum cleaner, iron and so on to be neatly stowed.

4 **Worktable and chair** Positioned in maximum natural light, the table, with its tubular construction, is adjustable in height. The chair, in matching style, neatly folds up when not in use.

5 **Wall unit** Simply and cheaply constructed, this ingenious unit opens out to provide an additional work surface and space for tools (see picture, left).

6 **Wardrobe** This second-hand buy has been painted to match the scheme and provides useful storage for dressmaking activities.

7 **Window treatment** A single curtain with eyelets, simply slotted on a wire, is the answer to prettying up this room and providing privacy after dark.

8 **Lighting** Two pendant lights with large reflective coolie shades come from an existing ceiling point and are redirected over work areas. A clip-on spot light provides directional lighting over the worktable.

Library

What luxury – a room dedicated to quiet contemplation, to academic pursuits, to pure pleasure! Even in these days of information technology, the book remains our vital link with history and other worlds, and whereas books are considered our 'friends', it is rare indeed to hear of anyone having a similar relationship with a personal computer. Although a library may be considered a workroom where serious research, study and perhaps writing are carried out, the title 'library' also conjures up a picture of an altogether more pleasurable space: warm and welcoming, a comfortable cocoon in which to while away the hours.

Your choice of colour scheme can do much to contribute to this feeling of cosseting. The selection of traditional, deep, jewel colours – ruby, sapphire and emerald – or warm earth tones – terracotta, sand, clay and volcanic rock – will give your room an intimate feeling (remember that dark warm colours advance: see pages 12–13) as well as suggesting security and tradition. Lining the walls, the books themselves may well provide the starting point to inspire your scheme. By echoing the colours of the book spines you will give your room a cohesive feel and you will create the illusion that the books are part of the structure of your room. The books themselves will provide plenty of interest, so you may opt to forgo strong patterns that may fight for your attention and distract from the 'stars' of the room. Instead you may like to concentrate on incorporating an interesting variety of textures. Imagine your shiny book spines against a background of dark green felt walls; rough natural seagrass flooring is underfoot, green-and-red plaid, heavy linen curtains grace the window and worn, glossy, red leather chairs stand in an inviting group. The picture is completed by a log fire blazing brightly in the grate.

Lighting can so easily enhance or spoil this wonderful ambience that you have gone to such trouble to create. The central pendant light is to be avoided –

it will flatten all the textures and you will lose all feeling of intimacy. Instead choose several individual lights positioned in the lower portion of the room – table lamps, desk lamps, standard lamps – all these fittings will create pools of light that will impart a warm feeling. It is also important for the shelves to be well lit so that books can be located, removed and examined on the spot. Ceiling-fixed recessed wall washers (see page 9) will bathe the shelves in light or, as an alternative, you might consider library lights fixed to the uprights of the shelving units themselves. Strip lights behind baffles, fixed within the bookcase, will highlight attractive books but are to be avoided if the bookcase is antique as the routing of wiring is likely to cause damage.

Of the furnishings in your library, a comfortable chair is paramount. This could be upholstered in either fabric or leather and needs to provide arm rests at a good height for reading comfortably. A high-backed chair (such as a wing chair) is wonderful for resting the head and for shielding the occupant from draughts. Positioned near a window, it will have the benefits of good natural light for reading and perhaps a pleasant view for idle moments. A foot rest will ensure perfect relaxation. It is also useful to include a desk and a more upright chair (possibly on castors) in your furniture arrangement. Other items that might be added include library steps to reach high-up books, a side table by your favourite chair to hold a lamp and possibly a drink, a coffee table to display decorative books and a magazine rack for current periodicals.

There are numerous methods of storing books and much will depend upon the layout and size of your room. By locating shelves around the perimeter of the room (not forgetting the dead area above the

Well-placed light fittings ensure that reading and writing are carried out in comfort in this cosy library.

doorways) you will maximize the space, but in a larger room bookcases can be utilized to divide the space into different zones for varying activities. When planning storage, remember that books come in all shapes and sizes, so allow for some extra-deep/tall spaces. For a more decorative look include ornaments on some shelves.

What style or theme could you choose for your library? One of the most popular is the 'gentlemen's club' look – lots of antique or reproduction furniture, club fenders before an open fire, leather upholstery with brass nailing, heavy velvet curtains and rich dark colours. Victorian and Edwardian styling includes many of these elements and would be a most suitable theme, especially if your house is of the period. But there is no reason why a more modern style could not be adopted for this room. Lighter colours, streamlined shelving and modern light fittings could give your library a totally different yet no less attractive appearance.

HOW THE ROOM MIGHT LOOK

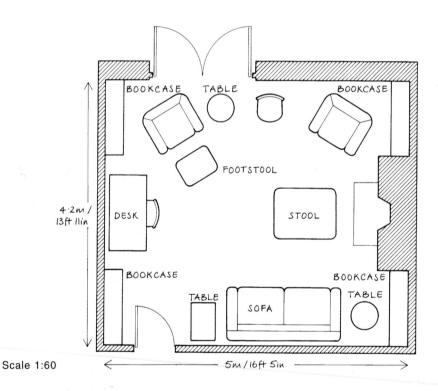

Scale 1:60   4·2m / 13ft 11in   5m / 16ft 5in

THE PLAN

Symmetry prevails in this relaxing library with bookcases flanking both the fireplace and the desk opposite. The summer reader's favourite spot is near to the French doors with a view of the garden. In winter the fireplace draws occupants to its side. A sofa offers additional seating.

DESIGN DECISIONS

1 **Scheme** Painted faux tortoiseshell walls form the background to this rich scheme. The same treatment extends over the ceiling and appears on woodwork to give the room a cohesive intimate look. Red upholstery introduces some warmth and the light beige flooring lifts the mood.

2 Flooring A plain beige, cut-pile carpet, fitted to close cover, ensures a hushed environment. A pretty floral needlepoint rug helps to break up the expanse of beige.

4 Bookshelves By having the same finish as the walls these bookcases appear to be part of the structure of the room and are far less intrusive than if they had been painted in a contrast.

3 Upholstery Comfort is the name of the game here. An upright chair at the desk ensures good support while writing and near the window a wing chair is just the shape to encourage a nap. A small footstool adds to the reader's comfort. In front of the fire (out of view) is a larger stool with a flat top to accommodate decorative books and the occasional tea tray. A small sofa along one wall offers extra seating and converts to a bed for the occasional guest.

5 Window treatment Full-length and luxuriously heavy, these curtains are sure to keep draughts at bay. The positioning of the curtain pole, high up above the French doors, contributes to a feeling of elegance.

6 Lighting Ceiling-fixed downlighters with gold baffles produce strong but warm pools of light, while table lamps and a swing-arm standard lamp pay deference to the traditional theme of the room. Pleated silk shades give out a soft diffused light.

INDEX

BOCA RATON PUBLIC LIBRARY

3 3656 0238348 7

2/19 warped. AJ

Photographic acknowledgements

The publishers have made every effort to contact copyright holders whose pictures are included in this book; however, omissions may inadvertently have occurred, and they will be pleased to hear from any copyright holder whose work is not properly acknowledged.

Camera Press Ltd 59, 90, 99, 103, 107, 119-20, Appleltoffl 38, Schneider 95, Symons 45; **Robert Harding Picture Library** Johnathon Pilkington 35; **Robert Harding Syndication** Henry Bourne/Homes and Gardens 70, Simon Brown/ Country Homes and Interiors 15, Marie Claire 53, Brian Harrison/Country Homes and Interiors 123, Homes and Gardens 55, 111, James Merrell/Homes and Gardens 123, Hugh Palmer/Country Homes and Interiors 30, Country Homes and Interiors (Designer: Stephen Ryan) 87, Brad Simmons 96; **Jane Nelson Associates** 47; **John Spragg** (Designer: David Hicks) 43, 51, 63, 66, 69, 83, 113; **Elizabeth Whiting Associates** 23, 27, 77, 79, 93, 114; **Henry Wilson** (Designer: Stephen Ryan) 75. Sketches on pages 76, 88-9 from designs by Stephen Ryan.

Measurement conversion chart

Inches

	0	1	2	3	4	5	6	7	8	9	10	11
Metres and millimetres												
0		25	51	76	102	127	152	178	203	229	254	279
1	305	330	356	381	406	432	457	483	508	533	559	584
2	610	635	660	686	711	737	762	787	813	838	864	889
3	914	940	965	991	1.016	1.041	1.067	1.092	1.118	1.143	1.168	1.194
4	1.219	1.245	1.270	1.295	1.321	1.346	1.372	1.397	1.422	1.448	1.473	1.499
5	1.524	1.549	1.575	1.600	1.626	1.651	1.676	1.702	1.727	1.753	1.778	1.803
6	1.829	1.854	1.880	1.905	1.930	1.956	1.981	2.007	2.032	2.057	2.083	2.108
7	2.134	2.159	2.184	2.210	2.235	2.261	2.286	2.311	2.337	2.362	2.388	2.413
8	2.438	2.464	2.489	2.515	2.540	2.565	2.591	2.616	2.642	2.667	2.692	2.718
9	2.743	2.769	2.794	2.819	2.845	2.870	2.896	2.921	2.946	2.972	2.997	3.023
10	3.048	3.073	3.098	3.124	3.150	3.175	3.200	3.226	3.251	3.277	3.302	3.327
11	3.353	3.378	3.404	3.429	3.454	3.480	3.505	3.531	3.556	3.581	3.607	3.632
12	3.658	3.683	3.708	3.734	3.759	3.785	3.810	3.835	3.861	3.886	3.912	3.937
13	3.962	3.988	4.013	4.039	4.064	4.089	4.115	4.140	4.166	4.191	4.216	4.242
14	4.267	4.293	4.318	4.343	4.369	4.394	4.420	4.445	4.470	4.496	4.521	4.547
15	4.572	4.597	4.623	4.648	4.674	4.699	4.724	4.750	4.775	4.801	4.826	4.851
16	4.877	4.902	4.928	4.953	4.978	5.004	5.029	5.055	5.080	5.105	5.131	5.156
17	5.182	5.207	5.232	5.258	5.283	5.309	5.334	5.359	5.385	5.410	5.436	5.461
18	5.486	5.512	5.537	5.563	5.588	5.613	5.639	5.664	5.690	5.715	5.740	5.766
19	5.791	5.817	5.842	5.867	5.893	5.918	5.944	5.969	5.994	6.020	6.045	6.071
20	6.096	6.121	6.147	6.172	6.198	6.223	6.248	6.274	6.299	6.325	6.350	6.375
21	6.401	6.426	6.452	6.477	6.502	6.528	6.553	6.579	6.604	6.629	6.655	6.680
22	6.706	6.731	6.756	6.782	6.807	6.833	6.858	6.883	6.909	6.934	6.960	6.985
23	7.010	7.036	7.061	7.087	7.112	7.137	7.163	7.188	7.214	7.239	7.264	7.290
24	7.315	7.341	7.366	7.391	7.417	7.442	7.468	7.493	7.518	7.544	7.569	7.595
25	7.620	7.645	7.671	7.696	7.722	7.747	7.772	7.798	7.823	7.849	7.874	7.899
26	7.925	7.950	7.976	8.001	8.026	8.052	8.077	8.103	8.128	8.153	8.179	8.204
27	8.230	8.255	8.280	8.306	8.331	8.357	8.382	8.407	8.433	8.458	8.484	8.509
28	8.534	8.560	8.585	8.611	8.636	8.661	8.687	8.712	8.738	8.763	8.788	8.814
29	8.839	8.865	8.890	8.915	8.941	8.966	8.992	9.017	9.042	9.068	9.093	9.119
30	9.144											

Feet (row labels)